Maria Fabricius Hansen

Übersetzungsfragen
Issues of Translation

Panofsky-Professur 2022
am Zentralinstitut für Kunstgeschichte München

Maria Fabricius Hansen

Übersetzungsfragen
Eine Neubewertung der Begriffe
›Renaissance‹, ›Antik‹ und ›Klassisch‹
in der Kunstgeschichte

Issues of Translation
'Renaissance', 'Antique', and
'Classical' Revisited

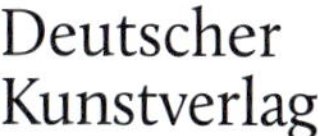

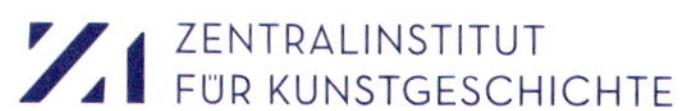

Die Panofsky-Professur
am Zentralinstitut für Kunstgeschichte

Will man Erwin Panofskys vielfältige Interessen und Forschungen auf nur einen Begriff bringen, dürfte die Auseinandersetzung mit dem ›Modell Antike‹ ein vielversprechender Vorschlag sein.[1] Nun beschäftigte die Frage nach der Rezeption antiker Kunst und Literatur zwar auch eine ganze Reihe andere, annähernd zeitgleiche Kunsthistoriker und Kunsthistorikerinnen nicht nur aus dem Warburg-Umkreis. Allein Panofsky ist es aber über 43 Jahren hinweg gelungen, für die Erforschung des ›Modells Antike‹ in der Kunst des Mittelalters und der Frühen Neuzeit in gleich mehreren Bereichen neue wissenschaftliche Standards zu setzen: von 1914, dem Veröffentlichungsdatum seiner Dissertation über Dürer, bis 1969, dem Jahr seiner letzten, posthumen Publikation.

Panofskys Spektrum deckt dabei *grosso modo* die Themenbereiche ab, die Aby Warburg nur am Rand berührt hatte. Anstatt die Pathosformel (wiederkehrende visuelle Topoi und ihre Bedeutungsverschiebungen) zu verfolgen, untersuchte Panofsky die Relevanz antiker kunsttheoretischer Texte für die Kunstliteratur und -praxis der frühen Neuzeit: zum Beispiel in seiner Arbeit über Dürers Kunstphilosophie sowie in seinem 1924 erschienenen Buch *Idea. Ein Beitrag zur Begriffsgeschichte der älteren Kunsttheorie.* Das Aufgreifen und Umformen antiker Themen und ikonographischer Traditionen behandelte er exemplarisch in der mit Fritz Saxl verfassten Studie zu *Dürers ›Melencolia I‹. Eine quellen- und typengeschichtliche Untersuchung*

The Panofsky Professorship
at the Zentralinstitut für Kunstgeschichte

If one sought to summarize in just one phrase the diverse interests and research of Erwin Panofsky, his examination into the 'model of antiquity' might come first to mind.[1] The question of the reception of ancient art and literature occupied a series of other art historians as well, including Panofsky's contemporaries in the Warburg circle. However, Panofsky alone succeeded in setting several new academic standards for research into the 'model of antiquity' in medieval and early modern art. He achieved this over a period of forty-three years: between 1914, when he published his dissertation on Dürer, and 1969, the year of his last posthumous publication.

The spectrum of Panofsky's work encompasses subject areas that his predecessor Aby Warburg had touched on only marginally. Rather than tracing the *Pathosformel* (recurring visual topoi and their shifts in meaning), Panofsky explored the relevance of ancient art-theoretical texts to art literature and practice in the early modern period – for example, in his work on Dürer's philosophy of art as well as his 1924 book *Idea. Ein Beitrag zur Begriffsgeschichte der älteren Kunsttheorie* (English translation published 1968 as *Idea. A Concept in Art Theory*). In his studies on *Dürers 'Melencolia I'. Eine quellen- und typengeschichtliche Untersuchung* (1923), written with Fritz Saxl, and *Hercules am Scheidewege und andere antike Bildstoffe in der neueren Kunst* (1930) he dealt in an exemplary manner with the adoption and transformation of ancient

(1923) und in *Hercules am Scheidewege und andere antike Bildstoffe in der neueren Kunst* (1930), um in der Folge das kunsthistorische Vorgehen zur Bedeutungs-Erschließung von Bildwerken in seinem berühmten dreistufigen Verfahren von Ikonographie und Ikonologie zu systematisieren. Schließlich entwickelte er aus einer erstmals 1944 vorgestellten Idee sein 1960 veröffentlichtes, vielleicht berühmtestes Buch *Renaissance and Renascences in Western Art*. Die deutsche Übersetzung wählt mit *Die Renaissancen der europäischen Kunst* leider einen Titel, der die entscheidende These unkenntlich macht: geht es Panofsky doch darum, die verschiedenen mittelalterlichen Rückgriffe auf die Antike (»renascences«) von der Renaissance des 15. und 16. Jahrhunderts kategorial zu unterscheiden. Damit kam die Diskussion, ob und wie es möglich sei, solche Epochenspezifika zu erfassen, die schon vor dem Zweiten Weltkrieg zentral diskutiert wurde, zu einem vorläufigen Ende.

Spätestens seit den 1980er Jahren freilich werden Panofskys Vorgehen und Schlussfolgerungen zunehmend kritisch betrachtet. Bemängelt wird eine Überbetonung von Texten, ein zu ›mechanisches‹ Deutungsverfahren angesichts der Eigenlogik und Ambivalenz von Bildern, eine Präferenz für neuplatonische Vorstellungen und die Epochenunterscheidung von Mittelalter und Renaissance aufgrund eines ›Disjunktionsprinzips‹: Laut Panofsky wurden im Mittelalter zwar auch antike Formen und antike Themen aufgegriffen, aber getrennt voneinander; dagegen konnte die spätere Forschung zeigen, dass dies nicht immer zutrifft. Ja, Panofskys Beschäftigung mit Renaissance und Antike wird nun auch als humanistischer Gegenentwurf, Kompensierungsversuch, wenn nicht als intellektuelle Fluchtbewegung angesichts der Gräuel von Nationalsozialismus und Zweitem Weltkrieg zu erklären versucht.[2]

Allein die Frage nach der spezifischen Antikenrezeption der Renaissance im Unterschied zu anderen Momenten und Formen der Auseinandersetzung mit antiken Modellen stellt

themes and iconographic traditions, before going on to systematize the art-historical procedure for analysing meaning in pictorial works through his renowned three-stage process of iconography and iconology. Finally, from an idea first presented in 1944, he developed what is perhaps his most famous book, *Renaissance and Renascences in Western Art*, published in 1960. The title of the German translation, *Die Renaissancen der europäischen Kunst*, unfortunately renders the book's decisive thesis unrecognizable: Panofsky's aim was to categorically distinguish the various medieval returns to antiquity ('renascences') from the Renaissance of the fifteenth and sixteenth centuries. With this study, Panofsky brought to a provisional close a discussion that had already been active before the Second World War, namely, whether – and if so, by what means – it was possible to capture such epochal specificities.

Since the 1980s at the latest, however, Panofsky's approach and conclusions have come under increasing criticism – whether for an overemphasis on texts; an overly 'mechanical' method of interpretation that fails to account for the inherent logic and ambivalence of images; or a preference for Neoplatonic ideas. Moreover, these criticisms have focused on the distinction Panofsky draws between the Middle Ages and the Renaissance based on a 'principle of disjunction', whereby ancient forms and ancient themes were taken up in the Middle Ages, yet separately from one another; indeed, as scholars have pointed out, there are already earlier examples of this being overcome. Panofsky's preoccupation with the Renaissance and antiquity is now often explained as a humanist alternative, if not an intellectual flight, in the face of the horrors of National Socialism and the Second World War.[2]

Only the matter of the specific reception of antiquity in the Renaissance – in contrast to other moments and forms of engagement with ancient models – continues to arise, itself experiencing a remarkable renaissance in recent years. One

sich weiterhin. Das Interesse daran und die Beschäftigung damit haben in den letzten Jahren ihrerseits eine bemerkenswerte Renaissance erfahren. Dazu zählen auch die Forschungen von Maria Fabricius Hansen, seit 2014 Professorin für Kunstgeschichte an der Universität Kopenhagen. Maria Fabricius Hansen hat ihre wissenschaftliche Karriere mit einer Studie zu Ruinenbilder im 15. Jahrhundert begonnen. Zwei 2003 und 2015 erschienene Bücher zur Bedeutung von Spolien und Spolienverwendung im frühchristlichen und mittelalterlichen Rom thematisieren den Umgang mit den antiken materiellen Relikten vorausgehenden Zeitraum. 2018 schließlich verfolgt sie mit einer großen Arbeit zur ›Grotesken-Mode‹ des späten 15. und des 16. Jahrhunderts eine zentrale Wiederentdeckung und breite Adaptation antiker Ornamentformen.

Maria Fabricius Hansen hat ihre Panofsky-Professur am Zentralinstitut für Kunstgeschichte München im Jahr 2022 nun dazu genutzt, die bereits für ihre vorausgehenden Forschungen zentralen Konzepte von ›Renaissance‹, ›Antike‹ und dem ›Klassischen‹ einer kritischen Revision zu unterziehen. Das Ergebnis legt sie mit dieser Publikation vor. Das Panofsky Fellowship in diesem Jahr wurde Antoine Gallay zuerkannt, der 2021 an der Universität Genf mit einer Arbeit zu *Sébastien Le Clerc (1637–1714). Entre arts et sciences: les ambitions d'un graveur au siècle de Louis XIV* promoviert worden war. Am ZI arbeitete Gallay an seinem neuen Projekt zu Zeichnung als epistemischer Praxis für die Wissenschaften zwischen 1650 und 1750.

Ermöglicht wurden beide Einladungen wie auch die vorliegende Publikation durch den Freundeskreis des Zentralinstituts für Kunstgeschichte München, die CONIVNCTA FLORESCIT e.V. Dieser großzügigen Förderung gilt unser aller Dank.

Ulrich Pfisterer

voice in the discussion is that of Maria Fabricius Hansen, Professor of Art History at the University of Copenhagen since 2014. Hansen began her academic career with a study of ruins in painting of the fifteenth century. Two books on the significance and use of spolia in early Christian and medieval Rome, published in 2003 and 2015, addressed the approach to and conceptualization of ancient material relics in the preceding period. Finally, in 2018, with a major work on the 'grotesques' of the late fifteenth and the sixteenth centuries, she examined the interaction of ancient ornamental forms with strategies of ambivalence.

As the 2022 Panofsky Professor at the Zentralinstitut für Kunstgeschichte, Munich, Hansen undertook a critical revision of the concepts of 'renaissance', 'antiquity', and the 'classical' already central to her previous research. She presents her findings in this publication. The 2022 Panofsky Fellowship was awarded to Antoine Gallay, who received his doctorate from the University of Geneva in 2021 with the dissertation *Sébastien Le Clerc (1637–1714). Entre arts et sciences: les ambitions d'un graveur au siècle de Louis XIV*. Gallay spent his time at the institute working on a new project concerning drawing as an epistemic practice in the sciences between 1650 and 1750. Both invitations, along with the present volume, were made possible by the Society of the Friends of the Zentralinstitut für Kunstgeschichte, the CONIVNCTA FLORESCIT e.V. We are all grateful for this generous support.

Ulrich Pfisterer

1 Alternativ wäre etwa auch an seine Auseinandersetzung mit Text-Bild-Verhältnissen zu denken.

2 Vgl. bereits Carl H. Landauer, »Erwin Panofsky and the renascence of the Renaissance«, in: *Renaissance Quarterly* 47 (1994): 255–281 und Konrad Hoffmann, »Panofskys ›Renaissance‹«, in: Bruno Reudenbach, Hrsg., *Erwin Panofsky* (Berlin, 1994): 141–144; oder etwa neuerdings Melis Avkiran, »Diffusion – Disjunktion – Distanz. Zur ideengeschichtlichen Ausrichtung eines kulturmorphologischen Prinzips in Erwin Panofskys ›Renaissance and Renascences‹ (1944)«, in: *Zeitschrift für Ästhetik und allgemeine Kunstwissenschaft* 64 (2019): 111–124.

1 Alternatively, one might consider his examination of text-image relationships.

2 Cf. Carl H. Landauer, "Erwin Panofsky and the Renascence of the Renaissance", in: *Renaissance Quarterly* 47 (1994): 255–281; Konrad Hoffmann: Panofskys "Renaissance", in: Bruno Reudenbach, ed., Erwin Panofsky, Berlin 1994: 141–144; or, more recently, Melis Avkiran, "Diffusion – Disjunction – Distance: On the Idea-Historical Orientation of a Cultural Morphological Principle in Erwin Panofsky's 'Renaissance and Renascences' (1944)", in: *Zeitschrift für Ästhetik und allgemeine Kunstwissenschaft* 64 (2019): 111–124.

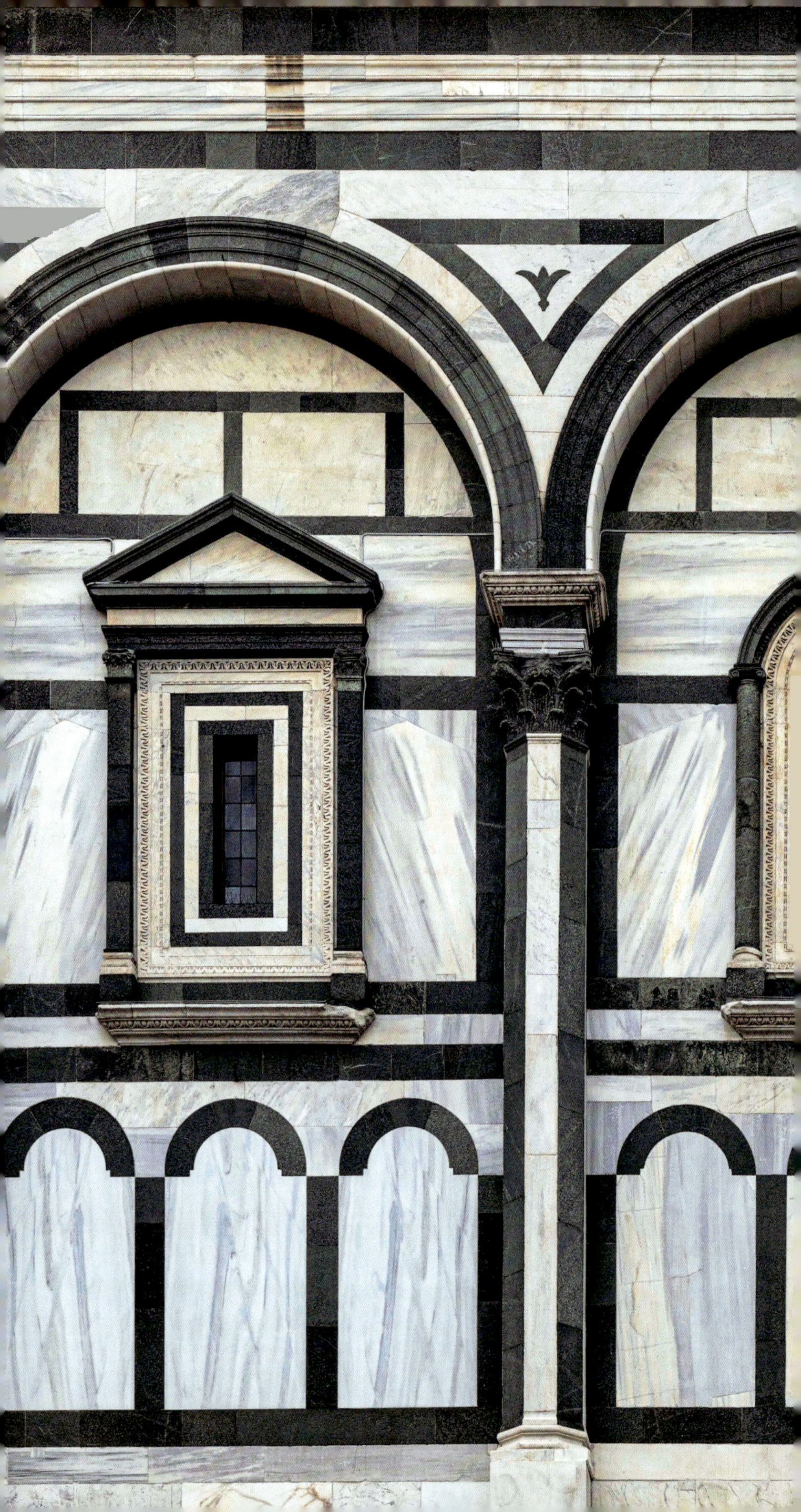

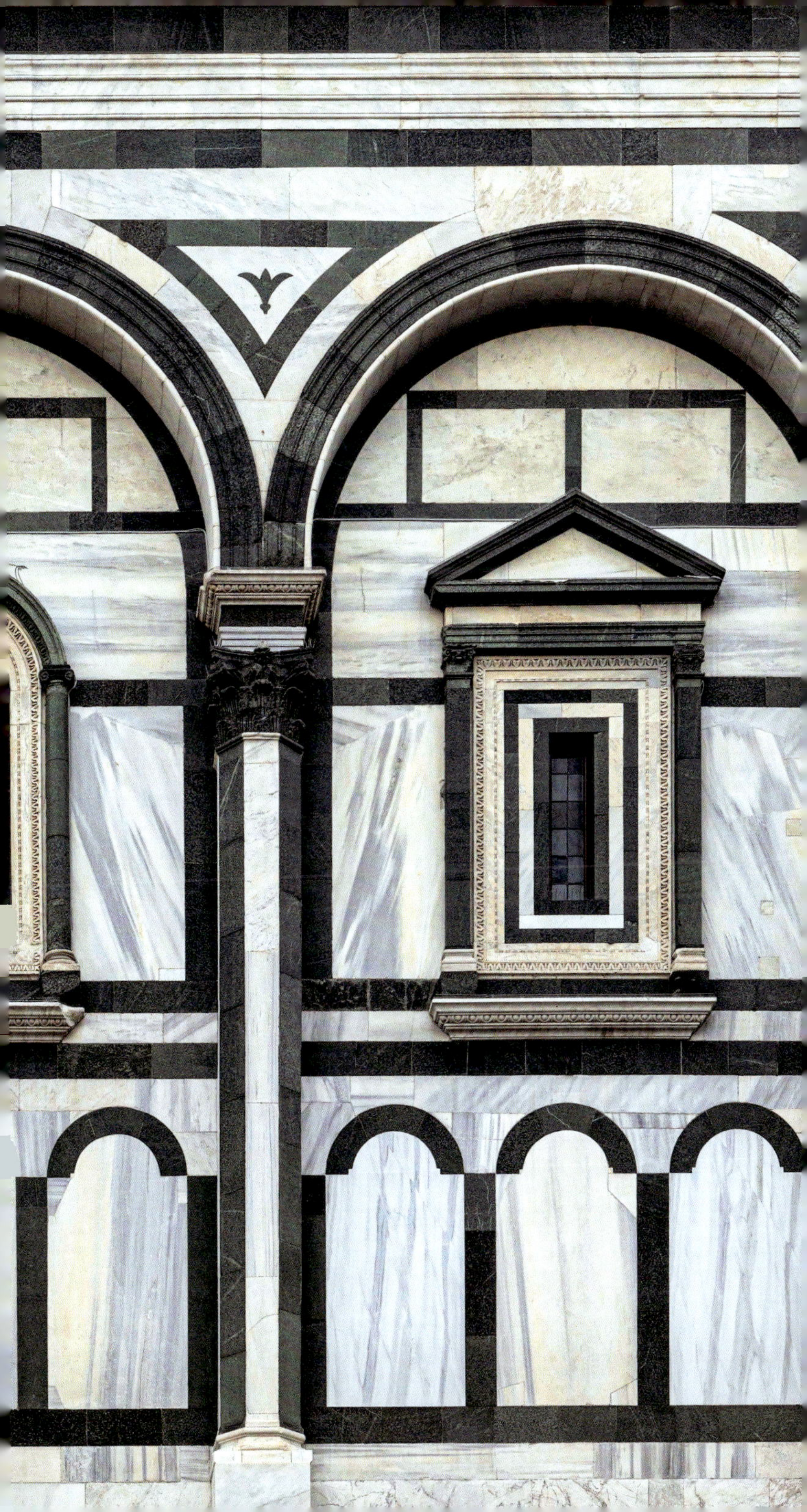

Maria Fabricius Hansen

Übersetzungsfragen
Eine Neubewertung der Begriffe ›Renaissance‹, ›Antik‹ und ›Klassisch‹ in der Kunstgeschichte

Der Nachweis von ›Renaissancen‹, d. h. von Epochen, in denen eine kulturelle Blüte mit einer Wiederbelebung der Antike in Zusammenhang gebracht wird, war ein zentrales Unterfangen der Kunst- und Architekturgeschichte der letzten beiden Jahrhunderte. Seit Jacob Burckhardt und andere Historiker des 19. Jahrhunderts das Konzept einer italienischen Renaissance etablierten, genießt die Epoche einen außerordentlich hohen Stellenwert innerhalb der Kunstgeschichte. Infolgedessen befassten sich Kunsthistoriker und Kunsthistorikerinnen mit der Definition zahlreicher anderer Renaissancen oder Wiederbelebungen bestimmter künstlerischer Formen und Inhalte, die mit der Antike in Verbindung stehen: eine byzantinische Renaissance, eine mit Papst Sixtus III. verbundene Renaissance im 5. Jahrhundert, eine karolingische Renaissance, eine Renaissance des 12. Jahrhunderts etc. Laufend werden Nachweise erbracht, dass auch das Mittelalter reich an Wiederbelebungen der Antike – und damit von Klassizismen – war. Im Allgemeinen gilt: Je mehr antike Einflüsse und je mehr Parallelen zur italienischen Renaissance in der Kunst anderer Länder oder Epochen aufgezeigt werden können, desto besser.[1] Dieser hohe Stellenwert der Antike und der Renaissance in der Kunstgeschichte bringt jedoch eine Reihe von Problemen mit sich, die Thema dieses Artikels sind.

Wo ist etwa das Ideal der klassischen Antike in der gemalten Architektur eines typischen Altarbildes der Mitte des

Maria Fabricius Hansen

Issues of Translation
'Renaissance', 'Antique', and 'Classical' Revisited

The identification of 'renaissances', in the sense of periods in which a cultural blooming is linked to a revival of antiquity, has been a major endeavour in art and architectural historiography of the last two centuries. Since Jacob Burckhardt and other nineteenth-century historians cemented the concept of the Italian Renaissance, this epoch has enjoyed an extraordinarily high status within the discipline. Consequently, art historians have sought to define numerous other revivals of antiquity at the level of artistic form and content: the Byzantine Renaissance, the Renaissance associated with Pope Sixtus III in the fifth century, the Carolingian Renaissance, the twelfth-century renaissance, and so on. Proving that the Middle Ages, too, were rich in revivals of antiquity – and, implicitly, in classicisms – has been an ongoing concern. Generally speaking, scholars have been eager to demonstrate influences from antiquity as well as parallels to the Italian Renaissance within the art of other times and places.[1] However, this high status of the antique and Renaissance periods within the narrative of art history involves a series of problems that I would like to address. Where, for instance, is the ideal of classical antiquity to be found in the painted architecture of a typical altarpiece from the mid-fifteenth century, like Domenico Veneziano's – in which slender, pointed arches in delicate shades of pink and light green frame the Virgin Mary and saints (Fig. 1)? And where are the similarities

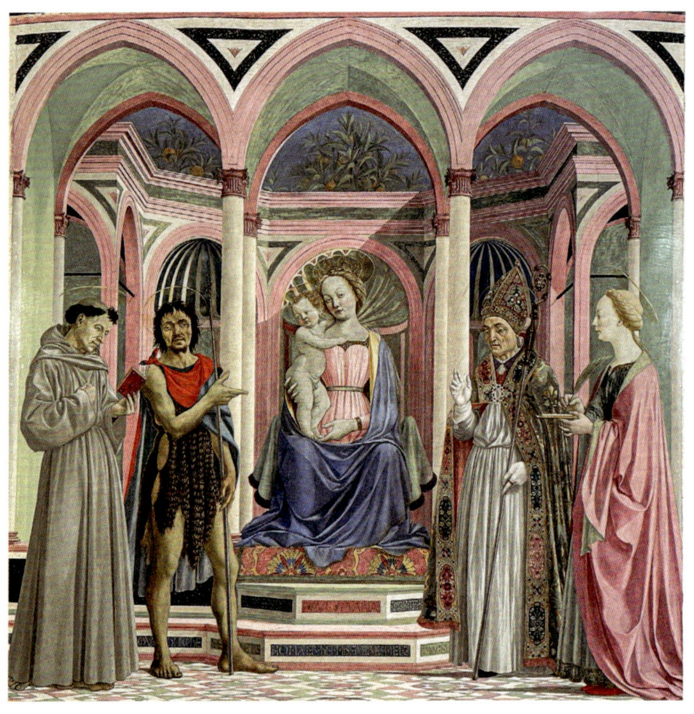

Abb. 1 Domenico Veneziano, *Madonna mit Kind und Heiligen*, ca. 1445,
Tempera auf Holz, 209 × 216 cm, Florenz, Gallerie degli Uffizi
Fig. 1 Domenico Veneziano, *Madonna with the Child and Saints*, c. 1445,
Tempera on wood, 209 × 216 cm, Florence, Gallerie degli Uffizi

15. Jahrhunderts von Domenico Veneziano, in der schlanke,
in zartem Rosa und Hellgrün gehaltene Spitzbögen die Jung-
frau Maria und die Heiligen einrahmen (Abb. 1)? Und wo
sind die Ähnlichkeiten zwischen der Kuppel des Florentiner
Doms, der von dem lange als großen Erneuerer der Antike bewunderten Filippo Brunelleschi entworfen worden ist, und
antik-römischen Bauten wie dem Pantheon (Abb. 2–3)?

Brunelleschis Kuppel ragt steil auf, ihre ziegelgedeckten
Dachflächen sind wie Stoffbänder zwischen den senkrechten
weißen Rippen gespannt. Bedingt durch die zweischalige
Bauweise bleibt ein Hohlraum zwischen dem Dach und dem

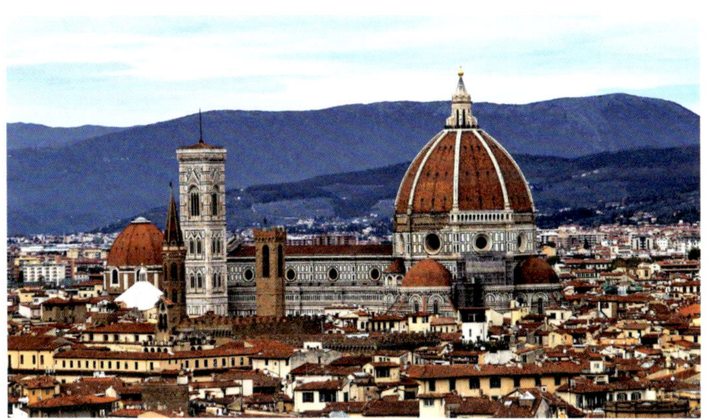

Abb. 2 Filippo Brunelleschi, Santa Maria del Fiore, Florenz, 1420–1436
Fig. 2 Filippo Brunelleschi, Cathedral, Florence, 1420–1436

between the dome of Florence Cathedral, designed by the alleged great reviver of antiquity, Filippo Brunelleschi, and ancient Roman buildings such as the Pantheon (Figs. 2–3)?

Brunelleschi's dome is rather steep, with almost textile-like fields of brick stretched out between the perpendicular white ribs. It was constructed using a double-shell approach, meaning that a void was left between the exterior roof and the interior of the dome, whereas the Pantheon is vaulted with a semicircle of solid concrete (Figs. 4–5). There are no formal or technical likenesses between the two solutions, between the verticality and white ribbing of Brunelleschi's double-shell structure and the hemispherical, compact dome of the Pantheon. – Whether consciously or unconsciously, the quest for revivals of antiquity and of the ideal of classicism has led scholars to purge from the canon such discordant, unclassical qualities of painted and built architecture of the fifteenth century. Moreover, not only have art historians extrapolated the classical to as many cultural periods as possible, but they have also tended to equate classicism, as a style, with artistic practices that draw inspiration from antiquity more generally.

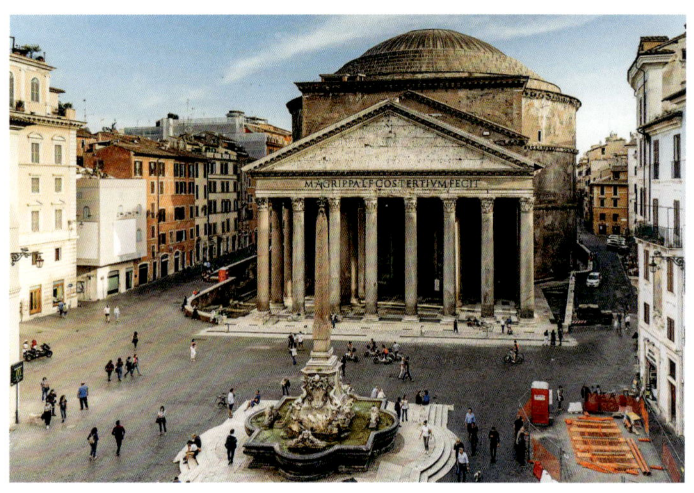

Abb. 3 Pantheon, Rom, ca. 126 n. Chr.
Fig. 3 Pantheon, Rome, c. 126 AD

Inneren der Kuppel, während das Pantheon mit einer Halb-
kugel aus massivem Beton überwölbt ist (Abb. 4–5). Es gibt
keine formalen oder technischen Ähnlichkeiten zwischen
den beiden Lösungen, zwischen der Vertikalität von Brunelleschis weißen Rippen und der doppelschaligen Struktur und
der halbkugelförmigen, kompakten Kuppel des Pantheons.
Das Streben nach Wiederbelebungen der Antike und das
klassizistische Ideal führten zu einer bewussten oder unbe-
wussten Reinigung, Zensur oder dem Übersehen solcher, in
dieser Sichtweise unstimmigen, unklassischen Qualitäten
der gemalten und gebauten Architektur des 15. Jahrhunderts.
Darüber hinaus extrapolieren Kunsthistoriker und Kunsthistorikerinnen das Klassische nicht nur aus möglichst vielen
Kulturepochen, sondern sie neigen auch dazu, den Klassizismus einerseits als Stil und andererseits als antikenbezogene
künstlerische Inspiration gleichzusetzen, obwohl sich diese
völlig unterschiedlich manifestieren können. In unserem
kunsthistorischen Kontext ist die Zweideutigkeit des Begriffs

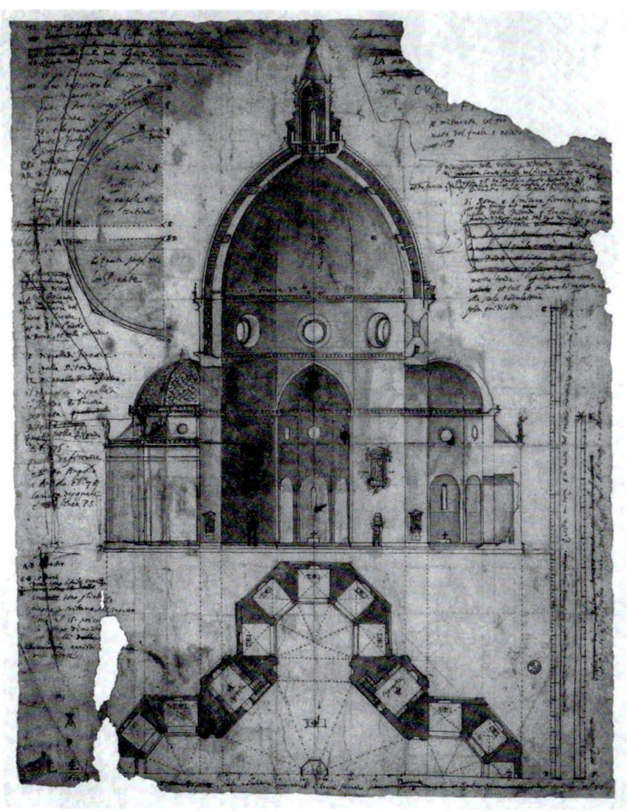

Abb. 4 Cigoli (1559–1613), Grundriss und Schnitt der Kathedrale von Florenz, Florenz, Gallerie degli Uffizi, Gabinetto dei disegni e delle stampe
Fig. 4 Cigoli (1559–1613), Section of the Florentine Cathedral, Florence, Gallerie degli Uffizi, Gabinetto dei disegni e delle stampe

In our art-historical context, the ambiguity of the term 'classical' is, indeed, a problem. In modern English, 'classical' designates both the overarching era of Greco-Roman antiquity and, more specifically, especially in archaeology, a subperiod within Greek antiquity. In the latter sense, classical Greek art is synonymous with the blooming of Athens at the time of Pericles and the construction of the Parthenon under the artistic direction of Phidias, in the fifth century BC. The

›klassisch‹ tatsächlich ein Problem. Im modernen Deutsch ist ›klassisch‹ eine Epochenbezeichnung – die griechische und römische Antike – aber auch, insbesondere in der Archäologie, eine Unterkategorie innerhalb der griechischen Antike. Der Begriff klassische griechische Kunst wird insbesondere in Bezug auf die Blütezeit Athens zur Zeit des Perikles und den Parthenon des Phidias im 5. Jahrhundert v. Chr. gebraucht. Die Engführung des ›Klassischen‹ und der Kultur des antiken Griechenlands und Roms wurde erst zu Beginn des 19. Jahrhunderts vorangetrieben, als sich die Kunstgeschichte als akademische Disziplin etablierte.[2] In seiner *Geschichte der Kunst des Altertums* (1764) verwendet Johann Joachim Winckelmann (1717–1768) den Begriff ›klassisch‹ noch keineswegs systematisch. Allerdings war Winckelmanns starke Betonung der Kultur des antiken Griechenlands zur Zeit des Perikles wirkmächtig. Diese Idealisierung wurde durch die Aufklärung, das Entstehen einer bürgerlichen Gesellschaft und die Entwicklung zur Demokratie in der nordwestlichen Welt vorangetrieben.

Die Tatsache, dass *klassisch* als Epochenmerkmal auch auf kunstgeschichtliche Epochen übertragen wurde, in denen ein bestimmter epochenübergreifender Stil, der als *Klassizismus* oder *klassizistisch* bezeichnet wird, vorherrschte, macht die Sache nicht einfacher. Als epochenübergreifende Stilbezeichnung hat Klassizismus keinen konkreten Bezug zu einer bestimmten Periode in der Kulturgeschichte des antiken Griechenlands und Roms. Ein bekanntes und einflussreiches Beispiel für einen solchen Begriffsgebrauch ist Heinrich Wölfflins Gegensatz zwischen Klassik (d. h. Renaissance) und Barock.[3] Wölfflin zufolge wird der Verlauf der Kunstgeschichte durch eine Dialektik von überwiegend klassizistischen und überwiegend unklassischen bzw. ›barocken‹ Perioden bestimmt. Diese Vorstellung von einer Kunstgeschichte, die sich durch bestimmte Strömungen und Gegenströmungen

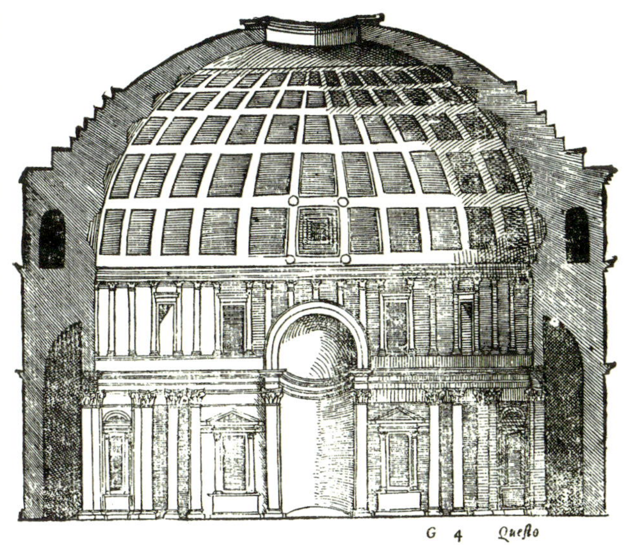

Abb. 5 Schnitt des Pantheons, 1540, Holzschnitt, in: Sebastian Serlio,
Le Antiqvita Di Roma. Tutte l'Opere d'architecttura et prospetiva (Buch III),
Venedig, S. 9
Fig. 5 Section of Pantheon, 1540, Woodcut illustration, in: Sebastian Serlio,
Le Antiqvita Di Roma. Tutte l'Opere d'architecttura et prospetiva (Book III),
Venice, p. 9

designation of the culture of ancient Greece and Rome as
'classical' did not become current until the early nineteenth
century, when art history was being established as an academic discipline.[2] Indeed, the term was not applied systematically even by Johann Joachim Winckelmann in his *History of
the Art of Antiquity (Geschichte der Kunst des Altertums)*, published in 1764. Winckelmann's account was nevertheless of
singular importance in idealizing the culture of fifth-century
BC Greece. This orientation was rooted in the rationality of
the Enlightenment, the emergence of a bourgeois society, and
the move towards democratic forms of governance in Western
Europe and North America at the end of the eighteenth
century.

konstituiert, ist in der Geschichte unserer Disziplin weit verbreitet und führte dazu, dass der Begriff Klassizismus auch auf moderne bzw. außereuropäische Kunstbereiche angewendet wurde und wird. Im Allgemeinen besteht unter Kunsthistoriker und Kunsthistorikerinnen jedoch die Tendenz, besonders in Bezug auf die italienische Renaissance, die Wiederbelebung der Antike mit einer Wiederbelebung klassizistischer Stilformen gleichzusetzen.

Die Renaissance nach Panofsky

Erwin Panofskys brillantes Werk *Renaissance and Renascences in Western Art*, erschienen 1960 im englischen Original, ist eine der akademischen Grundlagen dieses konventionellen Verständnisses der italienischen visuellen Kultur des 15. Jahrhunderts, die durch eine Wiederbelebung der Antike gekennzeichnet ist und mit einem neuen Klassizismus einhergeht.[4] Bis heute durchdringt Panofskys Sichtweise der Epoche viele kunsthistorische Arbeiten in diesem Bereich. In *Renaissance and Renascences* konstruiert Panofsky sorgfältig ein doppeltes Argument: Erstens, dass es prinzipiell möglich und sinnvoll ist, mit kunsthistorischen Periodisierungen wie der Renaissance zu operieren, die einen bestimmten Zeitabschnitt (vom 14. bis zum 16. Jahrhundert) bezeichnen und spezifische Merkmale aufweisen; Zweitens, dass die Renaissance, die ihren Ausgang in Italien nahm, eng mit einer Wiederbelebung der Antike verbunden und durch ein neues Geschichtsbewusstsein gekennzeichnet war. Dies führte eine zeitliche Homogenisierung von Kunst und Architektur, bzw. eine Einheit von Zeit und Ort im Sinne einer Integration oder Verschmelzung antik-römischer Inhalte mit einem antik-römischen oder klassischen Stil herbei. Diese Konzeptualisierung der Renaissance als eine Epoche, die durch ihren klassischen

What complicates matters is that 'classical', as a period designation, has been transferred to eras of art history in which a certain trans-epochal style, termed 'classicism' or 'classicist', has governed. When used in a trans-historical sense to describe a style, classicism has no relation to any specific period in the cultural history of ancient Greece and Rome. One renowned and influential example is the opposition Heinrich Wölfflin posed between the classical (meaning the Renaissance) and the baroque.[3] According to Wölfflin, the course of art history was characterized by a dialectic whereby predominantly classicizing periods alternated with others that were predominantly unclassicizing or 'baroque'; this notion of art history as constituted by certain trends and counter-trends has been pervasive in the history of art history and has even led to the application of the term 'classicism' to modern and extra-European artistic fields. However, particularly when it comes to the Italian Renaissance, art historians have tended to take for granted that the revival of antiquity involved a revival of a classicist artistic idiom as well.

The Renaissance According to Panofsky

Erwin Panofsky's brilliant *Renaissance and Renascences in Western Art*, published in 1960, provided one of the major academic foundations for this conventional understanding of fifteenth-century Italian visual culture as characterized at once by a revival of antiquity and by a novel classicism.[4] This view of the period still permeates many art-historical surveys. In *Renaissance and Renascences,* Panofsky carefully constructed a twofold argument. First, he upheld the utility of art-historical periodization as a tool for designating a specific segment of time via the identification of distinguishing traits, practices, etc. Second, he argued that the Renaissance began

Stil und ein klares Geschichtsbewusstsein definiert werden kann, sollte sich als überaus bedeutsam erweisen.

Mit seinem Buch wandte sich Panofsky gegen die aufkommenden dekonstruktivistischen Tendenzen, die Periodisierungen grundsätzlich ablehnten. Außerdem wollte er demonstrieren, dass sich die Renaissance grundlegend von den früheren Wiederbelebungen der Antike unterscheidet, die seine Kollegen und Kolleginnen aus der Mediävistik in diesen Jahren konstatierten, wie zum Beispiel eine Renaissance des 12. Jahrhunderts. Der Originaltitel *Renaissance and Renascences* verdeutlicht diese Unterscheidung zwischen dem, was Panofsky als die eigentliche Renaissance erachtete, und den verschiedenen Erscheinungsformen mittelalterlicher Wiederbelebungen der Antike, die er mit dem Plural *Renascences* bezeichnet. Aus Panofskys Sicht erklärt das, um das 15. Jahrhundert zu datierende neue Geschichtsbewusstsein, die Neuartigkeit und Einzigartigkeit der italienischen Renaissance.

Die Grundlage für Panofskys Konzeption der Renaissance reicht zumindest zu Giorgio Vasari zurück, der Mitte des 16. Jahrhunderts sein kanonbildendes Buch, die *Vite*, über das Leben und die Werke der Künstler veröffentlichte, oder sogar noch weiter in die Vergangenheit, etwa zu Lorenzo Ghiberti im 15. oder Petrarca im 14. Jahrhundert. Hier finden wir die ersten Zeugnisse von Menschen, die ihre eigene Zeit als einen Aufbruch aus einer dunklen Vergangenheit betrachteten, der durch die Wiederbelebung der exemplarischen Kunst der Antike ermöglicht wurde.[5] Um die Mitte des 19. Jahrhunderts verfestigte Jacob Burckhardt dieses Narrativ in *Die Cultur der Renaissance in Italien* (1860), indem er das rosige Bild der Renaissance als eine Zeit der erwachenden Erkenntnis popularisierte:

Im Mittelalter lagen die beiden Seiten des Bewusstseins – nach der Welt hin und nach dem Innern des Menschen selbst – wie

in Italy, was closely linked with the revival of antiquity, and demonstrated a new historical consciousness, factors which brought about homogenous temporalities in art and architecture: a unity of time and place, as well as an integration or merging of ancient Roman content with an ancient Roman or classical style. This concept of the Renaissance as a period defined by its classical style and by its lucid historical consciousness has proven to be powerful.

With his book, Panofsky confronted the deconstructivist tendencies of his day, which ran counter to periodization. Moreover, he sought to distinguish the early modern Italian case from the various preceding revivals of antiquity to which his medievalist colleagues were calling attention at the time, such as the twelfth-century renaissance. The title of Panofsky's book highlights his distinction between the 'Renaissance' proper and the various subcurrents of revival during the Middle Ages, which he termed 'renascences', in the plural. For Panofsky, it was the new historical consciousness that explained the novelty and singularity of the Italian Renaissance.

The foundation for Panofsky's image of the Renaissance dated back to Giorgio Vasari, who in the mid-sixteenth century published his great book, the *Vite*, on the lives and works of Italian artists, or even earlier, for instance, to the writings of Lorenzo Ghiberti in the fifteenth century or of Petrarch in the fourteenth century. In these sources, we encounter the first testimonies from authors who viewed their own time as a departure from the preceding dark period, as a new era that revived the exemplary art of antiquity.[5] By the mid-nineteenth century, Jacob Burckhardt cemented this narrative in *The Civilization of the Renaissance in Italy* (*Die Cultur der Renaissance in Italien*), published in 1860, in which he poetically promoted the image of the Renaissance as a period of dawning insight:

unter einem gemeinsamen Schleier träumend oder halbwach.
[...] In Italien zuerst verweht dieser Schleier in die Lüfte; es er-
wacht eine *objective* Betrachtung und Behandlung des Staates
und der sämmtlichen Dinge dieser Welt überhaupt; daneben
aber erhebt sich mit voller Macht das *Subjective*; der Mensch
wird geistiges *Individuum* und erkennt sich als solches.[6]

Burckhardts metaphorische Evokation eines Schleiers, der
das menschliche Erkenntnisvermögen im Mittelalter trübte
und sich in der Renaissance auflöste, entspricht auch Panofskys Verständnis der Epoche als durch eine neue, klarsichtige
Erkenntnis der historischen Distanz zur Antike gekennzeichnet. Bereits als junger Kunsthistoriker brachte Panofsky
seine wirkmächtige These von der Perspektive als symboli-
scher Form vor.[7] Aus seiner Sicht ermöglichte die zentral-
perspektivische Konvention in der Bildgestaltung objektive
Darstellung, aber auch die notwendige Distanz zum Darstel-
lungsgegenstand. Diese Interpretation des neuen, zentralper-
spektivischen Bildraums reformulierte Panofsky in verein-
fachter Form in seiner 1953 erschienenen Einleitung zu *Early
Netherlandish Painting*.[8] *Renaissance and Renascences* schreibt
die Idee fort, dass die visuellen Kunstwerke der Zeit auf objektiver Auseinandersetzung mit der Vergangenheit, insbesondere der klassischen Antike, beruhten.

Panofskys Beschäftigung mit der Frage, ob und wie die Renaissance von früheren Perioden des Mittelalters, die die Antike nachahmten, unterschieden werden kann, mündet in der
Behauptung, dass das Neue in der Zeit um 1400, also das, was
sie als wirkliche Renaissance ausmacht, die Vereinigung des
antiken Stils mit dem antiken Inhalt sei. Umgekehrt, also die
Ablehnung dessen, bezeichnet er letztlich als das Prinzip der
Disjunktion. Als Beispiel für die von Panofsky als Neuerung
der Renaissance hervorgehobene Vereinheitlichung kann
Botticellis *Venus* (Gallerie degli Uffizi, Florenz) dienen, da sie

In the Middle Ages both sides of human consciousness – that
which was turned within as that which was turned without –
lay dreaming or half awake beneath a common veil. [...] In
Italy this veil first melted into air; an *objective* treatment and
consideration of the State and of all the things of this world
became possible. The subjective side at the same time asserted
itself with corresponding emphasis; man became a spiritual
individual, and recognized himself as such.[6]

Burckhardt's evocation of the 'veil' of the Middle Ages –
which had blurred clear observation, before evaporating in
the Renaissance – underlies Panofsky's understanding of the
latter period as characterized by a new clear-sighted recogni-
tion of the historical distance from antiquity. Already as a
young man, Panofsky had advanced his powerful narrative of
perspective as a symbolic form.[7] There, he pointed to how the
perspectival convention in image making enabled an objective depiction while also implying the viewer's distance from
the represented object. Later, in 1953, he rewrote this interpretation of the visual culture of the time in a simplified
form in his introduction to *Early Netherlandish Painting*.[8] His
Renaissance and Renascences, of 1960, is a continuation of this
idea of the artists of the time as objective observers of the
past, particularly of classical antiquity.

Panofsky's analysis of whether the Renaissance could be
distinguished from earlier periods in the Middle Ages that
had been characterized by an imitation of antiquity is founded
on the assertion that the years around 1400 saw an unprece-
dented unification of antique style with antique content, i. e.
a rejection of what he dubbed the medieval "principle of
disjunction". The innovative unification Panofsky detected
in the Italian Renaissance is exemplified in Botticelli's *Venus*
(Gallerie degli Uffizi, Florence), showing the ancient Roman
goddess nude and in a posture similar to ancient Roman rep-

die römische Göttin nackt und in einer Haltung zeigt, die den
in der Renaissance bekannten antik-römischen Darstellungen ähnelt. In einer seiner zahlreichen wortgewaltigen Passagen erklärt Panofsky: »The Middle Ages had left antiquity
unburied and alternately galvanized and exorcised its corpse.
The Renaissance stood weeping at its grave and tried to resurrect its soul. And in one fatally auspicious moment it succeeded.«[9] Passagen wie diese illustrieren Panofskys Idee einer Periode, die durch ein selbstbewusstes Verhältnis und eine
selbstbewusste Distanz zur Vergangenheit definiert werden
kann und die von einem zwingenden Drang zur Wiederbelebung der antik-römischen Kunst ausgelöst wurde. In Anbetracht der Beispiele von Domenico Veneziano und Brunelleschi (Abb. 1–2) scheint es jedoch geboten zu sein, die
Behauptungen Panofskys hinsichtlich eines akkuraten Geschichtsbewusstseins, also des Vorhabens einer Wiederbelebung der Antike in den bildenden Künsten und der Architektur des 15. Jahrhunderts und schließlich die Herausbildung
eines klassischen Stils als größte Leistung der Zeit kritisch zu
hinterfragen. Im Folgenden soll das kunsthistorische Bestre-
ben, die Renaissance auf der Grundlage einer Wiederbelebung der Antike und ihres Geschichtsbewusstseins zu definieren, untersucht werden.

Da Panofskys Werk bereits viel Kritik erfahren hat, möchte
ich unterstreichen, dass es aus meiner Sicht eine zentrale,
vielleicht einzigartige Rolle im kunsthistorischen Kanon einnimmt. Seine Texte sind überaus eloquent, äußerst gelehrt
und Panofsky war stets darum bemüht, Vereinfachungen zu
vermeiden. Er antizipiert fast alle nur erdenklichen Ein-
wände gegen seine Thesen und geht ausführlich darauf ein.
So ist etwa die in den letzten Jahrzehnten aufgekommene
Kritik an seiner ikonographischen Methode viel mehr in
Bezug auf seine Nachfolger und Nachfolgerinnen zu sehen,
als auf seine erstaunlich nuancierten Analysen. Wenn man

resentations known at the time. In one of his many eloquent passages, Panofsky remarked that "[t]he Middle Ages had left antiquity unburied and alternately galvanized and exorcised its corpse. The Renaissance stood weeping at its grave and tried to resurrect its soul. And in one fatally auspicious moment it succeeded."[9] Comments like this one epitomized a notion of the period as definable by its self-conscious relation to and distance from the past, all triggered by an urge to revive ancient Roman art. However, as suggested by the examples of Domenico Veneziano and Brunelleschi (Figs. 1–2), it seems necessary to critically question these assertions of an accurate historical consciousness, along with the claim that fifteenth-century artists and architects sought to revive antiquity in their images and buildings; consequently, we may question whether a classical style can be seen as a main achievement of the time. In what follows, we shall examine this long-standing tendency within art history to define and characterize the Renaissance by its revival of antiquity and by its historical consciousness.

Panofsky's writings have been subjected to much critique, so perhaps I should begin by remarking that to me his works rank at the absolute top of the art-historiographical canon, rivalled by very few, if any at all. His scholarship is amazingly eloquent and erudite, and he continuously and discerningly avoided simplistic shortcuts. In his writing, he foresees and addresses practically all conceivable objections to his argumentation. The critique of his iconographic method in recent decades, for instance, is more justified when aimed at his epigones than at his own, remarkably nuanced analyses. Nevertheless, contemporary art history's increasing attention to the ideologies embedded in art-historical discourse makes it possible to question some of the assumptions behind the scholarship of the second half of the twentieth century, including that of Panofsky. The protagonizing of 'revivals' of

jedoch die gesteigerte Aufmerksamkeit der zeitgenössischen Kunstgeschichte für die unausgesprochenen ideologischen Vorannahmen des kunsthistorischen Diskurses in Betracht zieht, so müssen auch einige jener Prämissen hinterfragt werden, die der Kunstgeschichte der 2. Hälfte des 20. Jahrhunderts zugrunde liegen und damit auch dem Werk Erwin Panofskys. Die Annahme, dass *Wiederbelebungen* der Antike die Geschichte der nordwestlichen Kunst entscheidend prägten, war selbstverständlich als Panofsky sein Buch verfasste. Heute scheint diese jedoch weniger gerechtfertigt zu sein denn je. Das Narrativ wird zunehmend durch das mit Aby Warburg verbundene Konzept des *Nachlebens* verdrängt, das insofern für die zeitgenössische Kunsttheorie produktiv zu sein scheint, als es den Fokus auf die labyrinthischen Wege der Bildmotive durch die Jahrhunderte legt und damit von der Wiederbelebung von etwas Vergessenem oder Totem abrückt.[10] Die Idee einer Wiederbelebung, sofern sie einen klar definierten Ursprung in der Geschichte impliziert, wurde mittlerweile stark problematisiert, besonders in Anbetracht eines ununterbrochenen Interesses an der Antike im europäischen Mittelalter. Diese Gegenströmung zu früheren Bemühungen, die Rezeption der Antike zu kartographieren, entspricht einigen der Beobachtungen, die in diesem Essay präsentiert werden.

Kunsthistoriker und Kunsthistorikerinnen haben insbesondere Panofskys Behauptung kritisiert, dass die italienische Renaissance synonym mit einem klar definierten Geschichtsbewusstsein ist. Aus Sicht dieser Kritiker und Kritikerinnen ist das, was landläufig als Renaissance bezeichnet wird, von einer großen temporalen Komplexität geprägt.[11] Doch liegt der Fokus weiterhin stark auf dem Verhältnis zur Antike und nicht so sehr auf dem, was an den künstlerischen Praktiken der Zeit neu, anders und unabhängig von antiken Vorbildern war. Gemeinsam ist diesen Analysen auch der

antiquity within European art, which was self-evident when Panofsky wrote his book, seems less justified today. It is increasingly being replaced by the concept of *Nachleben* associated with Aby Warburg, a concept which appears to be productive for contemporary art theory, implying a focus on the labyrinthine trajectories of a motif through the centuries rather than on the revival of something forgotten or dead.[10] Especially in light of the fact that there was sustained interest in antiquity through the Middle Ages, scholars have problematized the very idea of revival, which implies a well-defined 'origin' in history. This counter-current to mapping the reception of antiquity corresponds to some of the observations presented in this essay. Art historians have challenged Panofsky's claim that the Italian Renaissance was synonymous with a well-defined historical consciousness. According to these voices, the art of what is customarily called 'the Renaissance' involved a great complexity of temporalities.[11] But these voices are predominantly focused on rethinking the period's relationship to antiquity and not so much on examining what was new, different, or unantique about the artistic practices of the time. They have thus approached the Renaissance largely as an era of renewal, bound up, in one way or another, with antiquity.

However, critical discussion of the very concepts of the Renaissance, the antique, and the classical, based on what fifteenth-century artists and architects actually tended to produce, may further adjust our notions of the visual culture and historical consciousness of the time. This art-historical approach helps temper the unconditional admiration for antiquity which emanates from the written sources. It may thus contribute to nuancing our impressions of the fifteenth century as a period characterized by unrelenting attempts to retrieve the lost qualities of ancient Rome.

Gedanke, dass die Renaissance eine Periode der Erneuerung war und dass diese Erneuerung letztlich auf dem Verhältnis zur Antike beruht.

Eine kritische Auseinandersetzung mit den Konzeptualisierungen der Renaissance, der Antike und des Klassizismus auf Basis dessen, was Künstler und Architekten zu dieser Zeit tatsächlich produzierten, kann als wichtiges Korrektiv unserer Vorstellungen von der visuellen Kultur und dem historischen Bewusstsein des 15. Jahrhunderts dienen.[12] Dieser kunsthistorische Ansatz wird den Eindruck einer bedingungslosen Bewunderung für die Antike, den schriftliche Quellen des 15. Jahrhunderts zweifellos nahelegen, abschwächen. Die gängige Vorstellung vom 15. Jahrhundert als eine Periode, die von unablässigen Versuchen geprägt war, die verlorenen Qualitäten des antiken Roms wiederzuerlangen, könnte dadurch verändert und nuanciert werden.

Was bedeutet *all'antica*?

In *Renaissance and Renascences* legte Panofsky eine gründliche Untersuchung schriftlicher Quellen vor, in denen er ein starkes Interesse an der Antike und Bewunderung für Kunstwerke feststellte, die in der so genannten *all'antica*-Manier ausgeführt wurden, d. h. in einem der Antike angenäherten Stil.[13] Diese Quellen stammen von Gelehrten, die wir mit einem späteren Begriff als Humanisten bezeichnen, und von den Meistern der Malerei oder des Bauwesens, die wir mit den ebenfalls modern konnotierten Begriffen Künstler und Architekten versehen. In diesen Quellen getroffene Aussagen von *all'antica* als Stilideal zählen zu Panofskys zentralen Argumenten für die Definition der Renaissance und die Behauptung ihres Ursprungs in Italien. Panofsky, der auf Englisch schrieb, übersetzte das italienische *all'antica* mit ›classical‹,

In *Renaissance and Renascences*, Panofsky presented a thorough survey of written sources in which he detected a strong interest in antiquity and an admiration for artworks executed in an *all'antica* manner, meaning in a style similar to that of antiquity.[12] These sources were written by learned scholars, who would later come to be called humanists, and by masters of painting or building, whom we designate – again using terms with modern connotations – artists and architects. The idealization of the *all'antica* style pronounced in these sources counted among Panofsky's main evidence for defining the Renaissance and claiming its origin in Italy. But a first problem arises already here, as he, writing in English, translated the Italian *all'antica* as 'classical'.[13] Remarkably, he did not discuss or qualify this understanding of the term. Although the regular Italian meaning of *antica* is simply 'old', his interpretation of *all'antica* as signifying a style inspired by classical Roman antiquity is typical of art-historical writings of the nineteenth and twentieth centuries through the present day. This problem of translation, and the blurred conceptualization that accompanies it, is largely caused by the common use of the word 'antiquity' in English and *Antike* in German and other European languages to designate the period of ancient Greece and Rome. The Italian word *antica*, however, encompasses not only this era but also later historical ones, for instance the Middle Ages.[14] When it came to periods of the remote past, artists and architects of the fifteenth century did not distinguish between one and the other; everything which dated back in time was 'antique'. In fact, Panofsky himself noted that *antica* literally only means 'old' in Italian, but he did not develop this observation towards problematizing his own claim that the artists sought to revive classical antiquity. Indeed, he maintained the assumption that their ideal of *all'an-*

was sich als Problem erweisen würde.[14] Es ist bemerkenswert, dass er diese Begriffsauffassung weder diskutierte noch definierte. Obwohl *antica* aus dem Italienischen schlicht mit ›alt‹ übersetzt werden müsste, ist Panofskys Auffassung von *all'antica* als Bezeichnung für einen von der klassischen römischen Antike inspirierten Stil typisch für kunsthistorische Schriften des 19. und 20. Jahrhunderts bis heute. Die Begriffsunschärfe, die durch dieses Übersetzungsproblem entsteht, ist insbesondere auf den gemeinsamen Gebrauch des Wortes ›antiquity‹ im Englischen und ›Antike‹ im Deutschen und anderen europäischen Sprachen als Epochenbezeichnung für das antike Griechenland und Rom zurückzuführen. Das italienische Wort *antica* deckt hingegen sowohl diese Wortbedeutung ab als auch spätere historische Perioden wie z. B. das Mittelalter.[15] Die Künstler und Architekten des 15. Jahrhunderts unterschieden nicht zwischen der einen oder der anderen Periode einer fernen Vergangenheit. In ihrem Denken war alles, was in der Vergangenheit lag, antik. Panofsky selbst stellte fest, dass *antica* im Italienischen wörtlich nichts anderes als alt bedeutet, aber er ging dieser Feststellung nicht weiter nach, um seine eigene Behauptung zu problematisieren, dass Künstler die Intention hatten, die klassische Antike wiederzubeleben. Er wich nicht von der Annahme ab, dass das Ideal der *all'antica* auf jene Periode bezogen ist, die wir heute als Antike definieren und die er als klassisch bezeichnet. Mit anderen Worten: In Panofskys Analyse verschmolzen das Klassische im Sinne der römischen Antike mit dem Klassischen im Sinne einer bestimmten stilistischen Ausdrucksweise. Im gesamten Buch verwendet er den Begriff ›klassisch‹ unterschiedslos als Epochenbezeichnung und als Bezeichnung für einen Stil. Für ihn war das *all'antica*-Ideal gleichbedeutend mit der ›klassischen Antike‹, obwohl im Italien des 15. Jahrhunderts mit den Begriffen *antica* oder *antico* genauso das Mittelalter gemeint war.[16]

tica related to the period we define as antiquity, the period he called 'classical'. In other words, Panofsky's analysis merged 'classical' in the sense of the ancient Roman period and 'classical' in the sense of a certain stylistic idiom. Throughout the book, he used the term interchangeably as a period designation and a designation of style. To him, the *all'antica* ideal was equivalent to 'classical antiquity', even if a fifteenth-century Italian, when talking about something that was *antica* or *antico*, was also referring to the medieval period.[15]

In his discussion of the historical consciousness of the Renaissance, Panofsky observed that Giorgio Vasari had reflected on the significance of the word *antico* and had suggested a distinction between *antico* and *vecchio*.[16] According to Vasari, *antico* signified the ancient or antique, while *vecchio* denoted the art and architecture that had come after the Roman Empire, which in Vasari's view had been made by Greeks.[17] The latter thus corresponds to 'Byzantine' or 'early medieval', in modern terminology. Nevertheless, even the theoretically sophisticated Vasari did not apply this vocabulary consistently throughout his writings. Moreover, the fact that Vasari found it necessary at all to provide guidelines for the meaning of the words 'antique' and 'old', *antico* and *vecchio*, reveals that the distinction between them was new at that moment, in the mid-sixteenth century, and would therefore have been unknown a century and a half earlier, at the time of, say, Brunelleschi.[18]

In fact, the use of *antico* to designate not only ancient Roman but also early Christian and medieval phenomena lingered even after Vasari. To mention an example from another cultural field: Cesare Vecellio, who authored a great volume on ancient and modern clothing, published in 1590, used the designation *antico* or *antica* for various historical periods (Fig. 6).[19] Vecellio labelled a dress *antica* whether it dated to Roman antiquity, to the period around the year 1000, or even

In seiner Diskussion des Geschichtsbewusstseins der Renaissance konstatiert Panofsky, dass Giorgio Vasari über die Bedeutung des Wortes *antico* nachdachte und eine entsprechende Unterscheidung zwischen *antico* und *vecchio* vorschlug.[17] In Vasaris Definition bedeutet *antico* altertümlich oder antik, während *vecchio* die Kunst und Architektur aus der Zeit nach dem Römischen Reich bezeichnet, die Vasari als griechische Kunst betrachtete.[18] *Vecchio* entspricht also dem, was wir in moderner Terminologie als byzantinisch und mittelalterlich bezeichnen. Doch selbst der theoretisch versierte Vasari wandte die eigene Terminologie in seinen Schriften nicht konsequent an. Außerdem zeigt die Tatsache, dass Vasari es für notwendig erachtete, Leitlinien für die Verwendung und Bedeutung der Worte *antico* und *vecchio* zu geben, dass deren Unterscheidung in der Mitte des 16. Jahrhunderts noch neu war. Es ist daher wenig plausibel, dass anderthalb Jahrhunderte früher, etwa zur Zeit Brunelleschis, diese Unterscheidung bereits getroffen worden wäre.[19]

Tatsächlich war die Verwendung des Begriffs *antico* zur Bezeichnung nicht nur der römischen Antike, sondern auch frühchristlicher und mittelalterlicher Artefakte auch noch nach Vasari gebräuchlich. Um ein Beispiel aus einem anderen kulturhistorischen Bereich zu nennen: In seinem 1590 publizierten monumentalen Werk über antike und moderne Kleidung verwendet Cesare Vecellio die Bezeichnung *antico* oder *antica* für verschiedene historische Epochen (Abb. 6).[20] Vecellio bezeichnet ein Kleid als *antica*, wenn es aus der römischen Antike oder aus der Zeit um das Jahr 1000 stammt, aber auch allgemein, wenn es mehr als ein paar hundert Jahre alt ist. Der ungewöhnliche Federhut einer *donna antica*, den er um das Jahr 1000 datiert, dient Vecellio auch als Beispiel für den Erfindungsgrad der Kleidung, die von Frauen in der Antike getragen wurde.

Was es in der Renaissance bedeutete, *all'antica* zu bauen oder zu malen, und der Begriff, den man sich von der Antike

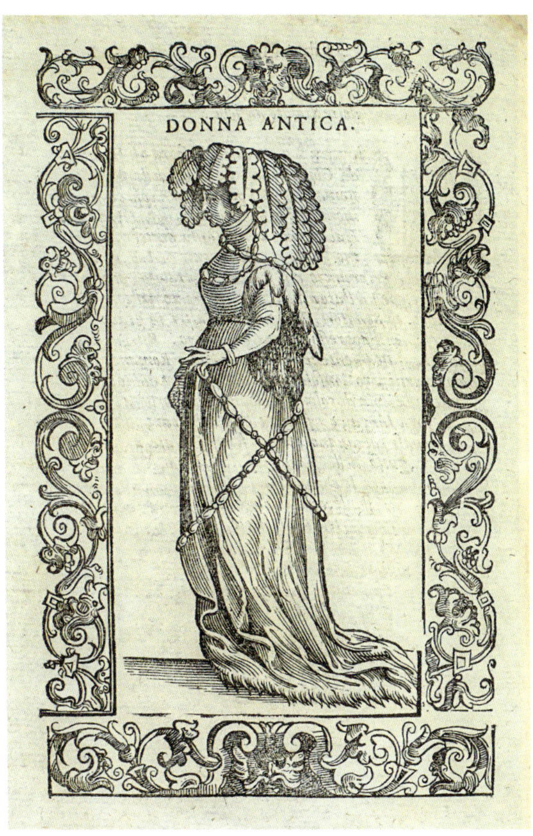

Abb. 6 ›Antica‹ als Bezeichnung für ein um 1000 datiertes Kleid bei Cesare Vecellio, in: ders., *De gli Habiti Antichi e Modérni di Diversi Parti di Mondo*, 1590, Venedig, Fol. 25v
Fig. 6 'Antica' as applied by Cesare Vecellio to women's dress, which he dates c. 1000, in: *De gli Habiti Antichi e Modérni di Diversi Parti di Mondo*, 1590, Venice, fol. 25v

to the more recent past. The amazing feathery hat of a *donna antica*, which he dated to around the year 1000, indicates the inventiveness of the dresses he imagined women to have worn in the ancient past.

The Renaissance's meaning of building or painting *all'antica*, and its concept of antiquity more generally, was certainly

machte, war zweifellos nicht identisch mit den Konzepten der ›Antike‹ und des Klassischen‹ des 20. Jahrhunderts, die durch Jahrhunderte der kunsthistorischen und archäologischen Forschung geprägt wurden. Wenn wir den modernen englischen Begriff *classical* als Synonym für *all'antica* verwenden, riskieren wir, den Menschen der Renaissance ein Antiken-Konzept zu unterstellen, das mehr oder weniger jenem entspricht, das sich bis zur Moderne herausbilden sollte, wobei die römische Antike dann ungefähr die Kultur der ersten Jahrhunderte vor und nach Christi Geburt bezeichnet. Im 15. Jahrhundert war archäologisches Quellenmaterial schwer zugänglich und wurde nur ansatzweise untersucht. Die Quantität und Qualität des Einblicks in das antike römische Kulturerbe damals kann nicht mit dem enormen Wissensfundus verglichen werden, der im Verlauf der Neuzeit und der Moderne durch die Einrichtung von Museen und Archiven verfügbar gemacht und durch die philologischen Bemühungen der letzten Jahrhunderte immens vertieft wurde. Auch Bildquellen wurden nur allmählich durch die Verbreitung von gedruckten Büchern zugänglich, was sich seit der Erfindung der Fotografie im 19. Jahrhundert beschleunigte. Es gibt keinen Grund dafür, an der tiefen Bewunderung des 15. Jahrhunderts für die *all'antica*-Manier zu zweifeln, aber eine Klärung dessen, was mit dem Wort *antica* überhaupt gemeint war, scheint noch immer geboten zu sein. Die folgende Untersuchung ist daher der Frage gewidmet, welche Vergangenheit Künstler und Architekten des 15. und frühen 16. Jahrhunderts in ihren Zeichnungen studierten und wie sie in der Folge tatsächlich bauten und malten. Der Fokus liegt dabei auf der Zeit, bevor die Verbreitung von gedruckten und illustrierten Büchern die Entstehung neuer stilistischer Paradigmen und Verbreitung historischen Wissens in dramatischer Weise vorantrieb.

not identical to the notions of 'antiquity' and the 'classical' that the twentieth century has developed from centuries of art-historical and archaeological research. If we use the modern English term 'classical' as synonymous with *all'antica*, we risk taking for granted that people of the past operated with a concept of antiquity similar to what we have come to know in modern times, where Roman antiquity roughly means the culture around the first centuries prior to and after the birth of Christ. In the fifteenth century, archaeological material was accessible only with difficulty and remained, for the most part, little investigated. In terms of both quantity and quality, the insight that people of the Renaissance gained into ancient Roman cultural heritage is therefore incomparable to the enormous corpus of knowledge that has become available with modern philological efforts and with the establishment of museums and archives. Visual representations of ancient works became accessible only gradually through the dissemination of printed, illustrated books, a process which accelerated with the invention of photography in the nineteenth century. While there is no reason to doubt the Renaissance's profound admiration for a good ancient style, it is still necessary to clarify what exactly they meant when they used the word *antica*. In the following inquiry into this, I shall focus on the period prior to the rise of printed and illustrated books, which dramatically altered paradigms of style and historical knowledge. We shall consider what past was studied by fifteenth- and early sixteenth-century artists and architects; how they undertook this study; and what they ultimately built and painted as a result.

Mittelalterliche Antike

Trotz der begründeten Skepsis, die der Brunelleschi-Spezialist Howard Saalman, aber auch Ernst H. Gombrich, Howard Burns und andere bereits vor Jahrzehnten formulierten, gehen viele Kunsthistoriker und Kunsthistorikerinnen nach wie vor davon aus, dass Brunelleschi die antike Architektur in Rom studierte und dass diese Beschäftigung große Auswirkungen auf sein architektonisches Schaffen in Florenz hatte.[21] Zwar führte ein jüngerer Trend in der Kunstgeschichte zu einer neuerlichen intensiven Auseinandersetzung mit den mittelalterlichen Quellen des 15. Jahrhunderts, doch wird in vielen Studien zur Kunst und Architektur der italienischen Renaissance nach wie vor die Standarderzählung wiederholt, dass Brunelleschis Begegnung mit dem Pantheon um 1420 seine Lösung des Problems der Gewölbekonstruktion der kolossalen Vierung der Florentiner Kathedrale inspiriert habe oder dass seine Studien der antiken Architektur in Rom ein Katalysator für die Erneuerung der Architektur in Florenz gewesen seien, die so zentral für den kunsthistorischen Kanon ist (Abb. 2–5).[22] Die Geschichte von Brunelleschis römischen Studien geht auf dessen anonymen Biographen, wohl Antonio Manetti, zurück, der die Vita des von ihm bewunderten Brunelleschi im späten 15. Jahrhundert verfasste, also lange nach Brunelleschis Tod im Jahr 1446. Giorgio Vasari übernahm diese Biografie in der Mitte des 16. Jahrhunderts für seine eigene Brunelleschi-Vita, die weite Verbreitung finden sollte. Manetti zufolge ging Brunelleschi, nachdem er 1401 den Wettbewerb für die Bronzetüren des Florentiner Baptisteriums gegen Lorenzo Ghiberti verloren hatte, zusammen mit seinem Freund Donatello nach Rom, wo sie »viele Jahre lang« studierten und Zeichnungen anfertigten.[23] Die Tatsache, dass Donatello zu diesem Zeitpunkt erst fünfzehn Jahre alt war, ließ schon früh Zweifel an der

Medieval Antiquity

Despite the articulate scepticism formulated already decades ago by the Brunelleschi specialists Howard Saalman, Ernst H. Gombrich, and Howard Burns, among others, many art historians continue to assume that Brunelleschi studied ancient architecture in Rome and that his engagement with the architecture of Roman antiquity had major consequences for his buildings in Florence.[20] Even while a recent trend within art history has brought renewed attention to the medieval sources consulted in the fifteenth century, many surveys of Italian Renaissance art and architecture continue to repeat the canonical narrative that Brunelleschi's encounter with the Pantheon prompted his solution, around 1420, to the problem of vaulting the colossal crossing of Florence Cathedral, or that his studies of ancient architecture in Rome catalysed the reformulation of architecture in Florence (Figs. 2–5).[21] The story of Brunelleschi's Roman studies is known from his anonymous biographer, supposedly Antonio Manetti, who wrote the *vita* of the admired architect in the late fifteenth century, long after the latter's death in 1446. This narrative saw wide dissemination, especially after it was reiterated by Vasari in his mid-sixteenth-century *Vite*. The story goes that when, in 1401, Brunelleschi lost the competition for the bronze doors of the Florence Baptistery to Lorenzo Ghiberti, he and his friend Donatello left for Rome, where they studied and made drawings "for many years".[22] The fact that Donatello would only have been about fifteen years old at that time has caused some reflection as to the validity of the account, but the common conclusion is that Manetti probably confused the dates and that the trip actually did take place, only somewhat later.

Given Rome's proximity to Florence, actually less than 300 km, which would amount to about a week's travel on foot, it is not unlikely that Brunelleschi made such a trip.[23]

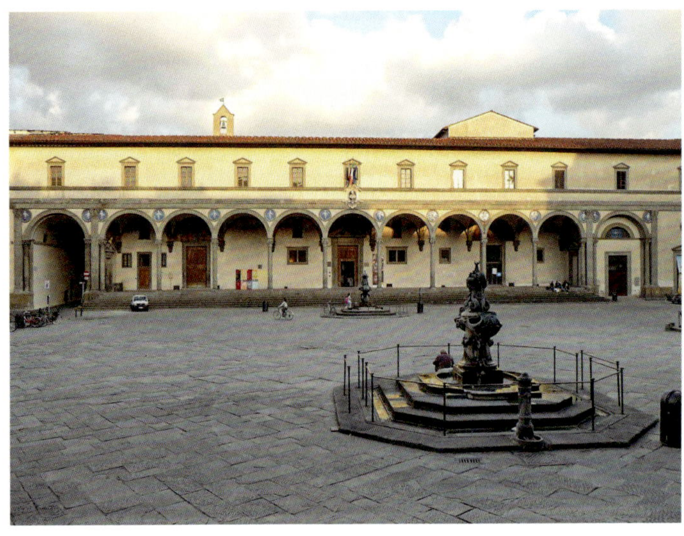

Abb. 7 Filippo Brunelleschi, Loggia des Ospedale degli Innocenti,
Florenz, begonnen 1419
Fig. 7 Filippo Brunelleschi, Loggia of the Ospedale degli Innocenti,
Florence, commenced 1419

Glaubwürdigkeit dieses Berichts aufkommen. Die allgemeine
Schlussfolgerung ist jedoch, dass Manetti die Daten verwech-
selt haben muss und die Reise dennoch stattfand, nur eben
etwas später.

In Anbetracht der geringen Distanz zwischen Rom und
Florenz, nämlich weniger als 300 km, was etwa einer einwö-
chigen Reise zu Fuß entspricht, ist es nicht unwahrscheinlich,
dass Brunelleschi eine solche Reise unternahm.[24] Es stellt sich
jedoch die Frage, wie hoch die Wahrscheinlichkeit ist, dass er
antike römische Architektur studierte und zeichnete und
dass er dadurch, wie in der Biografie behauptet wird, die
grundlegenden Prinzipien der antiken römischen Architektur, wie die klassischen Säulenordnungen, meisterte.[25] Ein
Vergleich der systematisch geordneten, filigranen Säulen
eines anderen Hauptwerks Brunelleschis, der Loggia des

The question, however, is whether he was likely to have studied and made drawings of ancient Roman architecture, such that, as the biography also claims, he came to understand the fundamental principles of ancient Roman architecture, among them the classical orders.[24] Comparison of the systematically ordered, delicate columns of another major work by Brunelleschi, the Ospedale degli Innocenti loggia, with an ancient Roman building – for instance, the Colosseum – demonstrates that Brunelleschi used columns in an unclassical manner (Figs. 7–8). Not only did his columns differ from classical Roman models in their slender proportions, but his application of this architectural element also ran counter to the practice of the ancient Romans, for whom columns always supported a horizontal entablature – a standard adopted from the Greeks. When the Romans added vaulted and arched structures to the Greek format, they employed square piers to support the arches. We see a merging of the Greek and Roman systems in the Colosseum, where the main structure consists of arches on square pillars; rather than serving a structural purpose, the trabeated columns are tacked onto the façade merely as a kind of ornament. If we look for precedents to Brunelleschi's combination of columns and arches, the models date to late antiquity and the medieval period, when masons deconstructed the classical system of columns supporting an entablature. Indeed, from the fourth century through the Middle Ages, the conventional ancient Roman coupling of columns and entablature was, on the whole, replaced by columns carrying arches (Figs. 9–10). As observed indirectly already by Vasari, who noted Brunelleschi's local Tuscan models, the architect did not have to venture all the way to Rome to find exemplars.[25] Eleventh- and twelfth-century buildings in Florence – such as the baptistery adjacent to the cathedral in the city centre, as well as the church of San Miniato al Monte – offered all the elements Brunelleschi needed

Ospedale degli Innocenti, mit antiken römischen Bauwerken, wie z. B. dem Kolosseum (Abb. 7–8), zeigt, dass Brunelleschi die Säulen auf sozusagen unklassische Weise einsetzte. Seine Säulen unterscheiden sich nicht nur durch ihre schlanken Proportionen von den klassischen römischen Vorbildern, er setzte sie auch anders ein als im antiken Rom üblich. Von den Griechen hatten die Römer die Norm übernommen, dass Säulen stets ein horizontales Gebälk tragen müssen. Als sie dieser griechischen Formel gewölbte und bogenförmige Strukturen hinzufügten, waren es stets rechteckige Pfeiler, die die Bögen trugen. Im Kolosseum wurde das griechische System mit dem römischen verschmolzen, oder besser gesagt, die architektonische Hauptstruktur besteht aus Bögen über rechteckigen Pfeilern. Die Halbsäulen dienen im Grunde als bloßes Architekturornament der Fassadengliederung und haben keine tragende Funktion. Mögliche architektonische Vorbilder für Brunelleschis Kombination von Säulen und Bögen stammen hingegen aus der Spätantike oder dem Mittelalter, als die Baumeister das klassische System von Säulen, die ein horizontales Gebälk tragen, hinter sich ließen. Ab dem 4. Jahrhundert und im gesamten Mittelalter wurde die konventionelle, altrömische Verbindung von Säulen und Gebälk durch Säulen ersetzt, die Bögen tragen (Abb. 9–10). Wie schon Vasari mit seinem Hinweis auf Brunelleschis lokale toskanische Vorbilder indirekt bemerkte, musste Brunelleschi nicht den weiten Weg nach Rom gehen, um vorbildhafte Architektur zu finden.[26] Gebäude aus dem 11. und 12. Jahrhundert wie das Baptisterium von Florenz, unmittelbar neben dem Dom und die Kirche San Miniato al Monte weisen sämtliche architektonische Elemente auf, die Brunelleschi für den Entwurf seiner Loggia benötigte.[27] So beruht die Fassadengliederung auf von Säulen getragenen Bögen, deren Proportionen mit den schlanken Säulen von Brunelleschis Loggia vergleichbar sind. Es überrascht daher nicht, dass auch Brunelleschi-Spezialisten

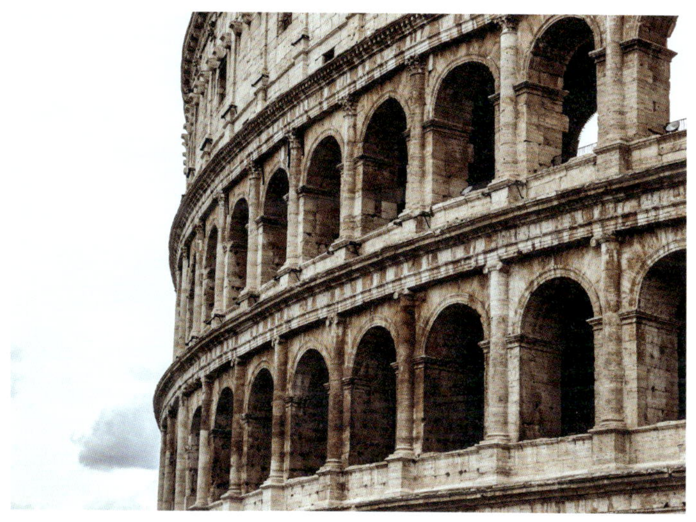

to design his loggia.[26] These included arches supported by columns, with slender proportions comparable to those of the columns of Brunelleschi's loggia. Brunelleschi specialists who were contemporaries of Panofsky in fact observed that nothing in the architect's built heritage either presupposes or requires a knowledge of ancient Roman structures. As one of these scholars, Gombrich, poignantly put it, in a 1967 article in which he pointed to Tuscan Romanesque structures as models for Brunelleschi: "What strikes us, in the vocabulary of quattrocento architecture, is less its classical character than its link with the medieval past".[27] In line with this, Howard Burns, in an influential article published in 1971, stated that "there is not a single major work of Brunelleschi for which a plausible and specific post-antique source (or sources) cannot be suggested".[28] As regards the conspicuous regularity and modularity of Brunelleschi's architecture, the obvious sources lie in the Gothic cathedrals of the fourteenth

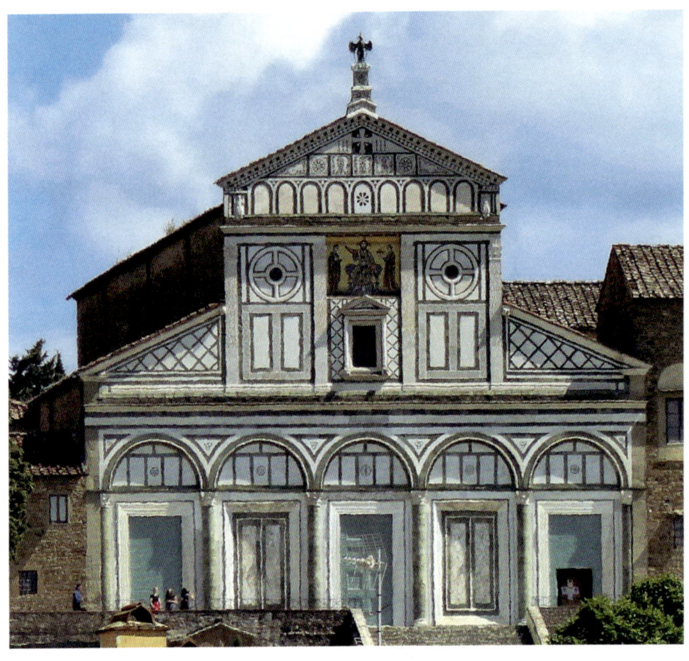

Abb. 9 San Miniato al Monte, Florenz, 11.–12. Jahrhundert
Fig. 9 San Miniato al Monte, Florence, eleventh–twelfth century

aus der Generation Panofskys immer wieder betonten, dass nichts in Brunelleschis architektonischen Werk Kenntnis der antiken römischen Strukturen voraussetzte oder erforderte. Einer der Kunsthistoriker, die feststellten, dass Brunelleschis Modelle der toskanischen Romanik entstammten, ist Gombrich (1967): »What strikes us, in the vocabulary of quattrocento architecture, is less its classical character than its link with the medieval past.«[28] In diesem Sinne stellte auch Howard Burns in einem einflussreichen Artikel von 1971 fest: »There is not a single major work of Brunelleschi for which a plausible and specific post-antique source (or sources) cannot be suggested.«[29] Was die auffällige Regelmäßigkeit und Modularität von Brunelleschis Architektur betrifft, so liegen die

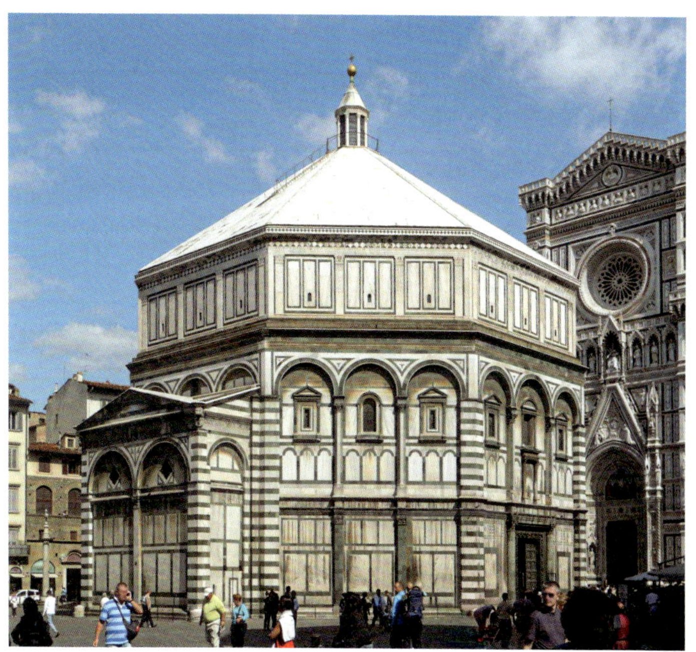

Abb. 10 Baptisterium, Florenz, 11.–12. Jahrhundert
Fig. 10 Baptistery, Florence, eleventh–twelfth century

century (Fig. 11). In fact, the Gothic obsession with numbers, proportions, and mathematics, as well as with optics and their Arabic theoretical foundations, not only paved the way for the architectural innovations of the fifteenth century but for the systematic development of linear perspective as well.[29]

These observations regarding Brunelleschi's dependence on his own recent past rather than on Roman antiquity have relevance also to the pictorial arts. One example is Masaccio, who modelled his representation of pilasters and Ionic columns for the architectural framing of *The Holy Trinity* (Santa Maria Novella) on a similar motif found on the interior wall of the baptistery (Figs. 12–13).[30] Indeed, the architecture represented in Florentine painting of the time does not come

offensichtlichen Vorbilder in den gotischen Kathedralen
des 14. Jahrhunderts (Abb. 11). Tatsächlich ebnete die gotische
Obsession mit Zahlen, Proportionen, Mathematik und
Optik – und ihre arabische theoretische Grundlage – nicht
bloß den Weg für die architektonischen Neuerungen des
15. Jahrhunderts, sondern auch für die systematische Entwicklung der Zentralperspektive.[30]

Die Beobachtung, dass Brunelleschi vielmehr auf die
künstlerische Tradition der eigenen jüngeren Vergangenheit
zurückgriff als auf jene der römischen Antike, kann auch für
die bildenden Künste geltend gemacht werden. Ein Beispiel
ist Masaccio, der in seiner Darstellung von Pilastern und io-
nischen Säulen in der architektonischen Umrahmung der
Dreifaltigkeit (Santa Maria Novella) ein Architekturmotiv aus
dem Inneren des Baptisteriums zitiert (Abb. 12–13).[31] Die florentinische Malerei dieser Zeit ist im Allgemeinen weit
davon entfernt, formale Aspekte antik-römischer Gebäude
zu repräsentieren. Domenico Venezianos bereits erwähnte
architektonische Umrahmung der Madonna und der Heiligen kann ohne weiteres als gotisierend bezeichnet werden
(Abb. 1). Die schlanken Säulen, die die Spitzbögen tragen,
sind selbst leicht spitz zulaufend, und die Polychromie der
Architektur folgt der toskanischen Tradition, in der nicht
nur weißer, sondern auch grüner und rosafarbener Marmor
zur Fassadengestaltung verwendet wurde. Giottos Campanile
für den Dom von Florenz ist ein bekanntes Beispiel für diese
Praxis (Abb. 2). Neben der Polychromie stimmen auch orna-
mentale Details mit dem Baptisterium überein, etwa die klei-
nen dreieckigen Felder über den Bögen von San Miniato und
dem Baptisterium, die sich in der gemalten Architektur von
Domenico Veneziano wiederfinden (Abb. 14–15).

Während die Affinität zu mittelalterlichen Quellen in
Architekturdarstellungen des 15. Jahrhunderts noch wenig
untersucht wurde, ist Brunelleschis Inspiration durch das

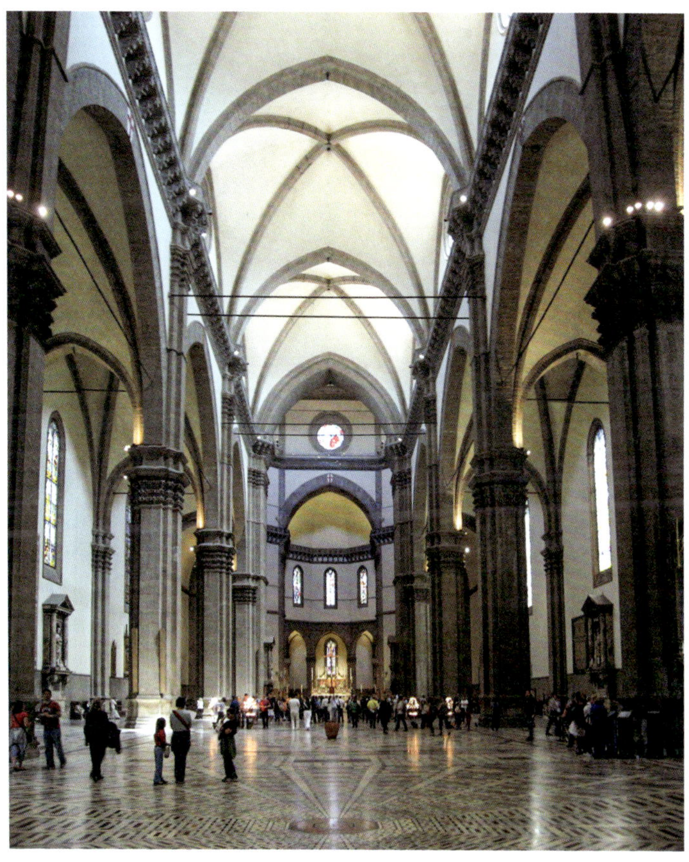

Abb. 11 Santa Maria del Fiore, Florenz, 14. Jahrhundert
Fig. 11 Santa Maria del Fiore, Florence, fourteenth century

close to displaying the formal aspects of ancient Roman buildings. As regards Domenico Veneziano's architectural framing of his Madonna and saints, the style can readily be described as Gothicizing (Fig. 1). The slender columns that bear the arches are slightly pointed, and the polychromy of the architecture is consistent with the Tuscan tradition, where not only white but also green and pink marbles were used in façade decoration. Giotto's campanile for the cathedral,

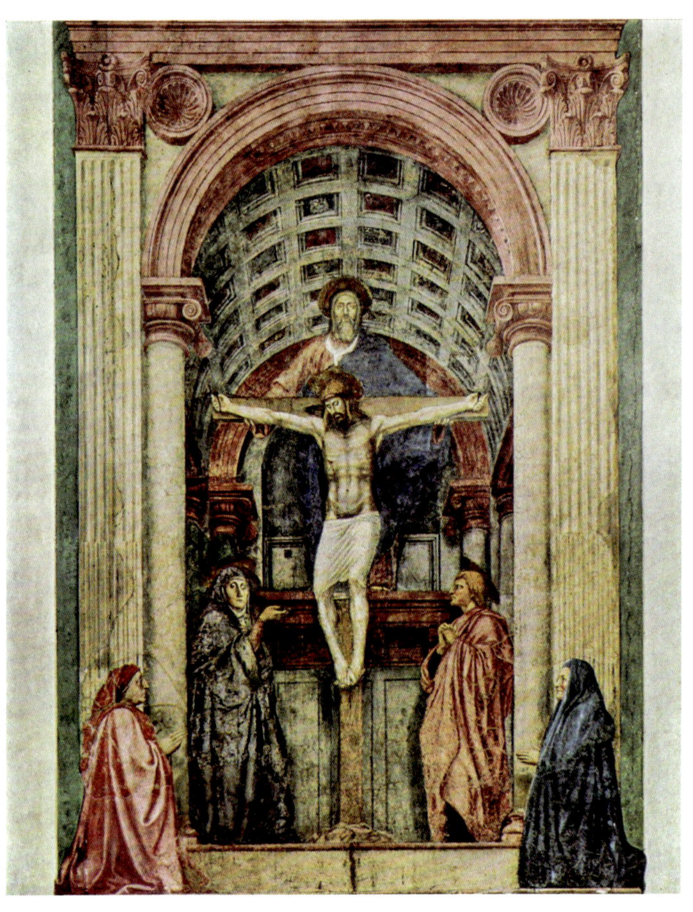

Abb. 12 Masaccio, *Dreifaltigkeit*, ca. 1426–1428, Florenz, Santa Maria
Novella
Fig. 12 Masaccio, *The Holy Trinity*, c. 1426–1428, Florence, Santa Maria
Novella

Baptisterium weithin anerkannt. Allerdings wird sie in der
Regel durch Argumentationslinien erklärt, die weiterhin
einige Probleme mit sich bringen. Das häufigste Argument
ist, dass Brunelleschi das Baptisterium nachgeahmt habe,
weil es für einen früheren antik-römischen Marstempel erachtet wurde, von dem einige behaupteten, er sei zur Zeit des

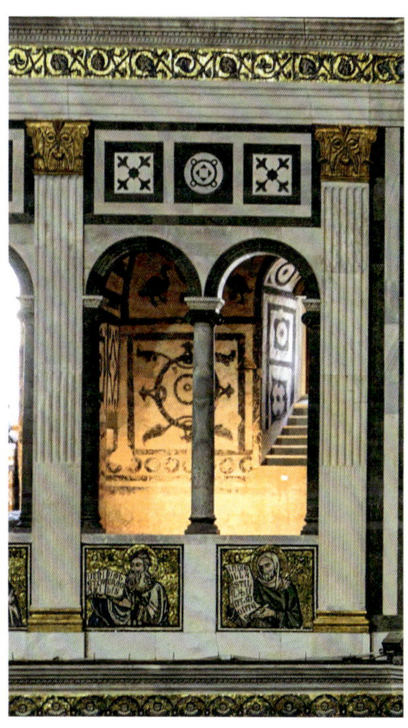

Abb. 13 Baptisterium, Detail des Innenraums: Von korinthischen Pilastern gerahmte ionische Säulen in der Galerie, 12. Jahrhundert, Florenz
Fig. 13 Baptistery, detail of the interior: Gallery arches with Ionic columns framed by Corinthian pilasters, twelfth century, Florence

immediately next to the Florence Baptistery, is a case in point (Fig. 2). In addition to the polychromy, even small ornamental details of Domenico Veneziano's painted architecture coincide with the façades of the baptistery and San Miniato, such as the small triangular fields above the arches (Figs. 14–15).

While such affinities with medieval sources in fifteenth-century representations of architecture have not received much attention, the inspiration Brunelleschi drew from the Florence Baptistery is widely recognized – albeit upheld by somewhat problematic lines of argument. Most

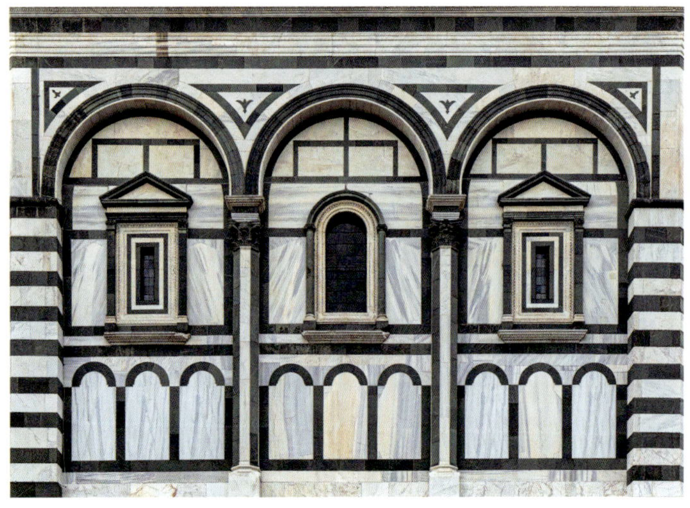

Abb. 14 Baptisterium, Florenz, Detail der Marmorverkleidung [Abb. 10]
Fig. 14 Baptistery of Florence, Detail of marble incrustation [Fig. 10]

Kaisers Augustus in nur fünfzehn Tagen Bauzeit errichtet worden.[32] Wenn Brunelleschi das Baptisterium jedoch auswählte, weil er darin einen antik-römischen Tempel erkannte, würde dies lediglich seine Intention bezeugen, die Antike wiederzubeleben; die tatsächlichen Inspirationsquellen bleiben jedoch nachantik.[33]

In seinem Artikel »From the Revival of Letters to the Reform of the Arts: Niccolò Niccoli and Filippo Brunelleschi« aus dem Jahr 1967 zeigt Gombrich deutliche Inspiration durch karolingische und insbesondere romanische Quellen des 12. Jahrhunderts bei den florentinischen Humanisten des 15. Jahrhunderts auf, die die Schriftarten der Manuskripte aus diesen Epochen als antik, *lettera antica*, bezeichneten. Dennoch zögerte Gombrich nicht, darauf hinzuweisen, dass es damals eine »concentration on classical studies« gegeben habe, und er stellte die Vermutung an, dass die Gelehrten, die die mittelalterliche Schrift als antik bezeichneten,

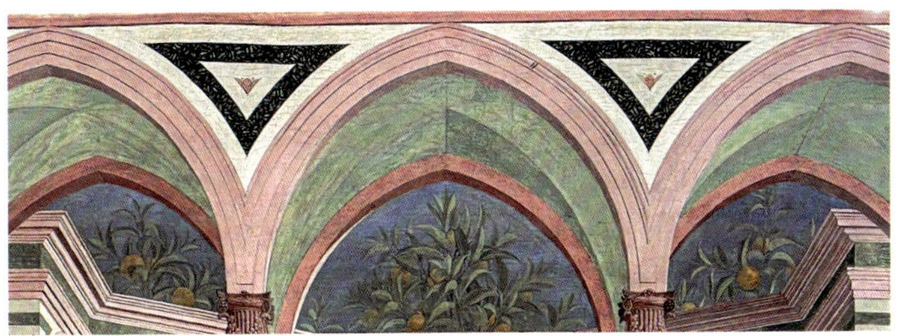

Abb. 15 Domenico Veneziano, *Madonna mit Kind und Heiligen*
(Detail: Ornamente in der gemalten Architektur), ca. 1445, Tempera auf
Holz, 209 × 216 cm, Florenz, Gallerie degli Uffizi [Abb. 1]
Fig. 15 Domenico Veneziano, *Madonna with the Child and Saints*
(Detail of ornament), c. 1445, Tempera on wood, 209 × 216 cm, Florence,
Gallerie degli Uffizi [Fig. 1]

frequent is the claim that Brunelleschi imitated the baptistery because it was thought to have originally been an ancient
Roman temple of Mars, ostensibly built at the time of the
emperor Augustus and erected in only fifteen days.[31] But if
Brunelleschi chose the Florence Baptistery because he iden-
tified it as an ancient Roman temple, this would only bear
witness to his *intention* to revive antiquity; his sources of inspiration, nevertheless, remain un-antique.[32]

In his article from 1967, "From the Revival of Letters to the
Reform of the Arts: Niccolò Niccoli and Filippo Brunelleschi",
Gombrich demonstrated the clear influence of Carolingian
and particularly of twelfth-century Romanesque sources on
the Florentine humanists of the fifteenth century, who des-
ignated the lettering of manuscripts from this period as 'antique', *lettera antica*. Nevertheless, Gombrich did not hesitate
to identify a "concentration on classical studies" during the
fifteenth century, and he suggested that the scholars who had
applied the label of 'antique' to the medieval lettering may
have believed it to be from ancient Rome.[33] He did not consider whether the Carolingian and Romanesque lettering

möglicherweise glaubten, sie stamme aus dem alten Rom.[34] Die Möglichkeit, dass die karolingische Schrift für die Menschen der damaligen Zeit schlichtweg antik war, wird genauso wenig in Betracht gezogen wie die Frage, ob es notwendig ist, die Übersetzung von *antica* dem Wortgebrauch im 15. Jahrhundert anzupassen, anstatt sie mit der römischen Antike in unserem heutigen Sinne synonym zu gebrauchen. Aus Gombrichs Sicht wurde Brunelleschis Reform der Architektur von Vorbildern des 12. Jahrhunderts inspiriert, weil diese eine Alternative zu den negativ besetzten Spitzbögen der Gotik und eine Vereinfachung oder Klärung der Stilsprache boten, die dem damaligen Zeitgeschmack entsprochen habe, wobei Gombrich spekuliert, dass Brunelleschi diese exemplarische Architektur, »which he probably invested with greater antiquity and more authority«, als authentisch antik erachtete.[35] In dieser Darstellung bleibt die ›echte‹ Antike also das unbestrittene Ideal und die künstlerische Sprache der *all'antica* entspricht einer »klassischen Norm«.[36] Auch Howard Burns stellte Brunelleschis vermeintliche Absicht die Antike (in unserem Sinne der Epochenbezeichnung) wiederzubeleben nicht in Frage, sondern argumentierte, dass Brunelleschi auf mittelalterliche Modelle zurückgriff, um die zugrundeliegenden Prinzipien zu extrahieren, wobei er zu dem Schluss kam, dass Brunelleschi tatsächlich als »revivor of much of the spirit of ancient architecture« angesehen werden kann.[37]

Architekturhistoriker, die der althergebrachten Darstellung von Brunelleschis antik-römischen Inspirationsquellen kritisch gegenüberstehen, haben seinen Rückgriff auf eine toskanisch-romanische Formensprache hingegen als bewusste nationalistische Aussage interpretiert.[38] Dies würde jedoch eine genaue Unterscheidung zwischen Epochen und Stilen voraussetzen, und es stellt sich die Frage, ob die textlichen und visuellen Zeugnisse des 15. Jahrhunderts den Schluss erlauben, dass die Menschen zu dieser Zeit die

would quite simply have been understood as 'antique' by the people of the day. Nor did he discuss whether it would be relevant to adjust the translation of *antica* to account for its fifteenth-century connotations, rather than simply equating it with Roman antiquity in our contemporary sense. To Gombrich, Brunelleschi's reform of architecture had been inspired by twelfth-century models because they offered him an alternative to the negatively charged, pointed arch of the Gothic period; moreover, these models represented a simplification or clarification of the stylistic language that people found appealing at the time. He suggested that Brunelleschi "probably invested [this exemplary architecture] with greater antiquity and more authority".[34] In this account, the 'real' antique period thus constituted the unquestionable ideal, and the *all'antica* artistic idiom remained synonymous with a 'classical norm'.[35] Similarly, Burns did not question that Brunelleschi's intention had been to revive antiquity – in our sense, as a period designation; however, he argued that it was the underlying principles that the architect had sought to extract (by using medieval models), concluding that Brunelleschi could readily be seen as a "reviver of much of the spirit of ancient architecture".[36]

Some architectural historians who have been critical of the old account of Brunelleschi's ancient Roman sources have interpreted his choice of a Tuscan Romanesque stylistic idiom as a deliberate, political, nationalistic statement.[37] But this would presuppose a precise distinction among periods and styles, and the question becomes whether the textual and visual testimonies substantiate the notion that people of the fifteenth century conceptualized the past in such comprehensive terms. In their *Anachronic Renaissance* (2010), Alexander Nagel and Christopher S. Wood argue that the Florentines were, indeed, well aware that the baptistery was a building from the eleventh century.[38] Nagel and Wood

Vergangenheit in einem solchen umfassenden Sinn konzeptualisierten. In *Anachronic Renaissance* (2010) argumentieren Alexander Nagel und Christopher S. Wood, dass die Florentiner und Florentiner der Renaissance durchaus wussten, dass das Baptisterium ein Bauwerk des 11. Jahrhunderts war.[39] Nagel und Wood argumentieren im Sinne eines Konzepts der Substitution, demzufolge es unerheblich war, ob das Baptisterium ›original‹ antik war oder als späterer Ersatz für ein antikes Gebäude errichtet wurde.[40] Mit ihrem Konzept gehen Nagel und Wood davon aus, dass die Künstler und Gelehrten der Renaissance nicht daran interessiert waren, zwischen dem, was wir heute als Mittelalter bezeichnen, und dem, was wir als römische Antike definieren, zu unterscheiden. Allerdings lässt ihre Beschreibung des Substitutionsprinzips in Bezug auf Vasari und Brunelleschi die Nachahmung der ›echten‹ Antike als das ungebrochene Ideal der Künstler und Architekten jener Zeit erscheinen: »The hypothesis of substitutability allowed Brunelleschi and Vasari to *look through* the eleventh- and twelfth-century buildings of Florence to the true meaning hiding behind them, namely, the normativity of the ancient Roman building manner«.[41]

Ich möchte hingegen eine Vereinfachung vorschlagen, indem ich anerkenne, dass der Antikenbegriff im 15. Jahrhundert praktisch allumfassend war; wobei zu beachten ist, dass die Menschen damals tatsächlich die Modelle des 11. und 12. Jahrhunderts den antik-römischen vorzogen. Das bedeutet, dass das Baptisterium in der Renaissance nicht aufgrund einer falschen Datierung als *antico* bezeichnet wurde, sondern gemäß der Terminologie bzw. der breiten und umfassenden Wortbedeutung jener Zeit tatsächlich antik war. Wenn der Florentiner Giovanni Rucellai, der als Förderer Leon Battista Albertis bekannt ist, Brunelleschi als »risucitatore delle muraglie antiche alla romanescha« bezeichnete, so bedeutet dies lediglich, dass Brunelleschi das »wiederbelebte«, was zu jener

operate with the concept of substitution, arguing that for the Florentines of the Renaissance it was irrelevant whether the baptistery was an 'original' antique or a substitution for an antique building.[39] With this concept, they propose that Renaissance artists and scholars were not interested in distinguishing between the 'medieval period' and the era of 'ancient Rome', as we designate them today. However, the observation that the substitution principle "allowed Brunelleschi and Vasari to *look through* the eleventh- and twelfth-century buildings of Florence to the true meaning hiding behind them, namely, the normativity of the ancient Roman building manner" continues to situate the imitation of 'real' antiquity as the dominant aim of Renaissance artists and architects.[40]

I would rather suggest a simplification in terms of acknowledging that the fifteenth-century concept of antiquity was practically all-inclusive, to which I would add the observation that the period preferred the eleventh- and twelfth-century models to the ancient Roman ones. This means that the Renaissance labelling of the baptistery as *antico* was not a misdating, as it actually was 'antique' in their broad, inclusive meaning of that word. When the Florentine Giovanni Rucellai, known as the patron of Leon Battista Alberti, referred to Brunelleschi as a "risucitatore delle muraglie antiche alla romanescha", he merely meant that Brunelleschi had revived what, at that time, was considered the good, ancient style of building.[41] This does not mean that Brunelleschi revived the manner of the buildings we today define as antique. The explanation that artists imitated the baptistery due to their *misdating* of it as a temple of Mars, moreover, leaves unexplained the question of why Brunelleschi and others also drew inspiration from San Miniato al Monte, although there was no tradition of backdating that church to Roman antiquity. But again, this is only an issue from a contemporary point of view, in which we operate with a conception of periodization and

Zeit als guter, antiker Baustil galt.[42] Es bedeutet nicht, dass Brunelleschi in einem Stil gebaut hat, der Gebäuden entspricht, die wir heute als antik bezeichnen. Der Erklärungsversuch, dass die Künstler das Baptisterium aufgrund einer falschen Datierung als Marstempel nachgeahmt hätten, lässt zudem die Frage offen, warum Brunelleschi und andere sich auch von San Miniato al Monte inspirieren ließen, obwohl in diesem Fall keine Tradition einer Rückdatierung in die römische Antike existierte. Doch auch das ist nur aus heutiger Sicht ein Problem, da wir mit modernen Konzepten von Periodisierung und Antike arbeiten, die für die Menschen in Florenz im 15. Jahrhundert irrelevant waren. Die Tatsache, dass Leon Battista Alberti gerade San Miniato al Monte als einen herausragenden »Tempel« bezeichnete (ein Begriff, der sowohl in lateinischen als auch in italienischen Texten der Zeit regelmäßig für Kirchen verwendet wurde), zeigt, dass selbst theoretisch versierte und historisch umfassend gebildete Gelehrte und Architekten der Zeit die toskanische Architektur des 12. Jahrhunderts hoch schätzten.[43]

Dass Sebastiano Serlio in seinem dritten Buch über die römischen Altertümer (*Le Antiqvita Di Roma*, 1540) nicht nur Bauten aus dem antiken Rom berücksichtigte, sondern auch zeitgenössische Architektur (von Bramante) einbezog, zeugt von einem Verständnis von *antico* als einer von der römischen Antike unabhängigen Stilkategorie.[44] Zu diesZeit vollzog sich jedoch bereits ein entscheidender Wandel, der das Verständnis der Epochenbezeichnungen ›Antike‹ und ›Mittelalter‹ erstmals in die er Nähe der modernen Begriffe bringen sollte. Obwohl Vasari noch die konventionelle Erzählung vom Baptisterium als antikem Tempel tradierte, wies er ausdrücklich auf den mittelalterlichen Ursprung von Brunelleschis anderen Inspirationsquellen hin, etwa der florentinischen Kirche Santi Apostoli aus dem 11. Jahrhundert. In Bezug auf diese Kirche hielt sich Vasari zwar an die florentinische Tradition,

of antiquity irrelevant to a fifteenth-century Florentine. That Leon Battista Alberti highlighted precisely San Miniato al Monte as a favourite 'temple' – a term regularly used to describe churches in both Latin and Italian texts of the time – shows that even the theoretically most advanced and most learned scholars and architects of the time cherished the Tuscan architecture of the twelfth century.[42]

Sebastiano Serlio's treatise – specifically, the third book, on Roman antiquities (*Le Antiqvita di Roma*, 1540) – included not just buildings from ancient Rome but also contemporary architecture (by Bramante). Again, this bears witness to an understanding of *antico* as a stylistic category independent of Roman antiquity.[43] By this time, however, decisive changes were occurring in the understanding of the period designations 'antiquity' and the 'Middle Ages', moving them towards something comparable to our modern concepts. Although Vasari still propagated the conventional designation of the Florence Baptistery as an ancient temple, he was explicit about the medieval origin of Brunelleschi's other sources of inspiration, such as the eleventh-century church of Santi Apostoli. In fact, Vasari adhered to the local convention of attributing this church to Charlemagne (echoing Manetti's survey of architectural history), but in our context it is his acknowledgement of its medieval origin that is crucial.[44] According to Vasari, Brunelleschi appropriated this medieval model because its stylistic value was equivalent to that of precedents from antiquity.[45] This observation aligns with Vasari's novel reflections on the distinction between 'antique' and 'old' and points both to a gradual abolishment of the all-inclusive concept of antiquity that had been sufficient in the fifteenth century and to a growing tendency towards periodization, which, as we shall return to shortly, had its final breakthrough in the nineteenth century.

ihre Gründung Karl dem Großen zuzuschreiben (unter Rückgriff auf Manettis Überblick über die Architekturgeschichte), doch in unserem Zusammenhang ist seine prinzipielle Anerkennung ihres mittelalterlichen Ursprungs entscheidend.[45] Aus Vasaris Sicht eignete sich Brunelleschi dieses mittelalterliche Modell an, weil es dem bewundernswerten Stil der Antike nahe kam.[46] Vasaris Beobachtungen entsprechen also seinen Überlegungen zur Unterscheidung zwischen antik und alt und weisen auf eine allmähliche Erosion des allumfassenden Antikenbegriffs hin, der im 15. Jahrhundert noch unbedenklich gewesen war, sowie auf eine wachsende Tendenz zur Periodisierung, die, wie wir sehen werden, im 19. Jahrhundert ihren endgültigen Durchbruch erleben sollte.

Post-klassische Ästhetik

Wenn wir uns den schriftlichen Quellen des 15. Jahrhunderts zuwenden, sehen wir anhaltende Bewunderung für frühchristliche und mittelalterliche Bauwerke, die unabhängig von historisch korrekten Identifizierungen ist. Giovanni Rucellai kann als ein typischer Vertreter dieser allgemeinen Tendenz ins Feld geführt werden. Rucellai besuchte Rom im Jubiläumsjahr 1450 und notierte in seinem Tagebuch, dass er einige Wochen damit verbrachte, vormittags die großen Basiliken zu besichtigen, während er nachmittags die antiken Bauten der Stadt erkundete: »quelle muraglie antiche et cose degne di Rome«.[47] In unserem Zusammenhang ist es bemerkenswert, dass er sich besonders für Gebäude wie die frühchristliche Santa Costanza interessierte (Abb. 16). Rucellais Bewunderung für Santa Costanza war insbesondere auf die Mosaike des Innenraums bezogen, die er als die schönsten der Welt bezeichnet.[48] Zu Rucellais Zeit wurde Santa Costanza oft als ehemaliger Bacchustempel identifiziert; die

Post-Classical Aesthetics

If we turn our attention to the written sources of the fifteenth century, we encounter a persistent admiration for early Christian and medieval buildings, regardless of any correct historical identification. The writings of Giovanni Rucellai may serve as a representative of this general trend. Rucellai visited Rome in the jubilee of 1450 and noted in his diary that, over a couple of weeks, he spent the mornings paying tribute to the major basilicas, and the afternoons seeking out the ancient structures of the city, "quelle muraglie antiche et cose degne di Rome".[46] In our context, it is noteworthy that he was particularly fond of buildings such as the early Christian Santa Costanza (Fig. 16). There, Rucellai's favourite feature was the mosaics adorning the interior, which he deemed the most beautiful in the whole world.[47] At the time, Santa Costanza was largely considered to be a temple of Bacchus.[48] The perception of such an early Christian structure as antique parallels that of the Florence Baptistery as a temple of Mars. In fact, early Christian and medieval churches were frequently understood to have been pagan temples in their original function, as in the case of the sixth-century Santo Stefano Rotondo in Rome, which was called a temple of Faun.[49] These identifications were caused by the lost remembrance of the buildings' timelines and past uses. The anecdotal explanations that developed throughout the medieval period substituted former knowledge and proved resilient.

In line with his appreciation of the mosaics of Santa Costanza, Rucellai greatly admired the cosmatesque, exquisitely decorated cloister of San Paolo fuori le Mura, from around 1200 (Fig. 17). He expressed no reservations towards the thoroughly unclassical use of columns and orders featured therein. Indeed, he ranked the cloister as *bellissimo* (most beautiful), explicitly praising the coupled columns

Wahrnehmung dieses frühchristlichen Bauwerks als antik ist also analog zur Bezeichnung des Baptisteriums in Florenz als Marstempel.[49] Tatsächlich gibt es zahlreiche Beispiele für frühchristliche und mittelalterliche Kirchen, die als ursprünglich heidnische Tempel erachtet wurden, wie z. B. die Kirche Santo Stefano Rotondo in Rom aus dem 6. Jahrhundert, die als früherer Tempel des Faunus galt.[50] Diese Identifizierungen sind auf die Unterbrechung der Überlieferung von ursprünglichen Funktionen und Errichtungsdaten der Gebäude zurückzuführen. Anekdotische Erklärungen, die im Laufe des Mittelalters entstanden sind, um die im Laufe der Jahrhunderte gewachsenen Wissenslücken zu schließen, hielten sich hartnäckig.

Nicht weniger als Giovanni Rucellai die Mosaiken von Santa Costanza schätzte, bewunderte er auch den im Kosmati-Stil dekorierten Kreuzgang von San Paolo fuori le mura aus der Zeit um 1200 (Abb. 17). Gegenüber der völlig unklassischen Verwendung von Säulen im Kreuzgang äußerte er keinerlei Vorbehalte. Tatsächlich bedachte er den Kreuzgang sogar mit dem Superlativ »bellissimo«, lobte ausdrücklich die bogentragenden Doppelsäulen und bewunderte die Raffinesse, »gentileze«, der Kosmati-Mosaike, die er ausführlich beschrieb.[51] Im Allgemeinen zeigt sein Tagebuch eine ausgeprägte Vorliebe für lichtreflektierende, vielfarbige Mosaike und andere Arten von Dekoration, die die Schwere eines Gebäudes optisch aufzulösen vermögen. Er schätzte Bauten aus frühchristlicher und mittelalterlicher Zeit nicht bloß, sondern scheint sie der ganz gegensätzlichen Materialität und Körperlichkeit der antik-römischen Bauten, die er nicht mit den gleichen Superlativen und Ausdrücken der Bewunderung versah, sogar ästhetisch vorgezogen zu haben.[52] Rucellai und seine Zeitgenossen betrachteten und kommentierten die antiken römischen Ruinen zweifellos mit Ehrfurcht, wobei sie besonders deren Monumentalität und Größe, die dafür

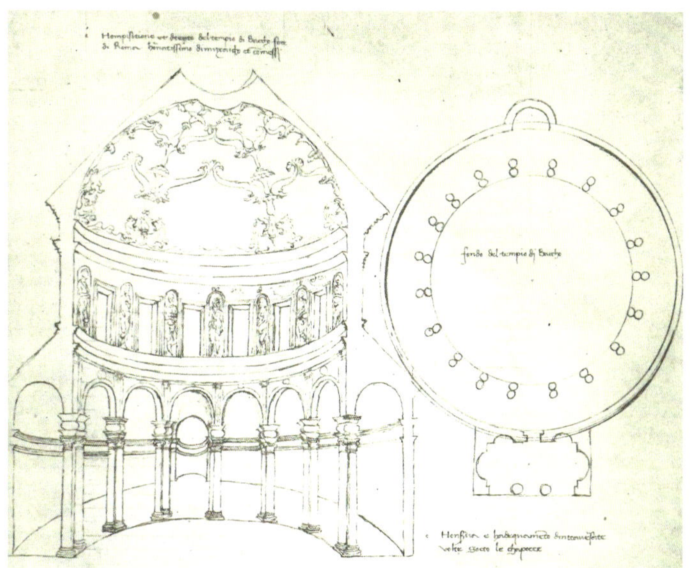

Abb. 16 Francesco di Giorgio, Grundriss und Schnitt des »Bacchustempels«, die damals gebräuchliche Bezeichnung für das Mausoleum des 4. Jahrhunderts, Rom, Santa Costanza, Mitte der 1480er Jahre, in: *Codex Saluzziano* 148, Turin, Biblioteca Reale, Fol. 88r (Detail)

Fig. 16 Francesco di Giorgio, Section and plan of the "Temple of Bacchus", the common designation of the time of the fourth-century mausoleum, Rome, Santa Costanza, mid 1480s, in: *Codex Saluzziano* 148, Turin, Biblioteca Reale, fol. 88r (detail)

carrying arches, along with what he called the *gentileze* (refinements) of the cosmatesque mosaics, which he described in detail.[50] In general, his diary reveals a marked preference for the reflection of light, polychrome mosaics, and other types of decoration whose visual effects tend to dissolve the solidity of a building. More than just appreciating architecture from the early Christian and medieval periods, he seems to have even preferred it aesthetically to the opposing materiality and corporeality of the ancient Roman structures, to which he did not ascribe such positively charged adjectives.[51] Rucellai and his contemporaries undeniably observed and

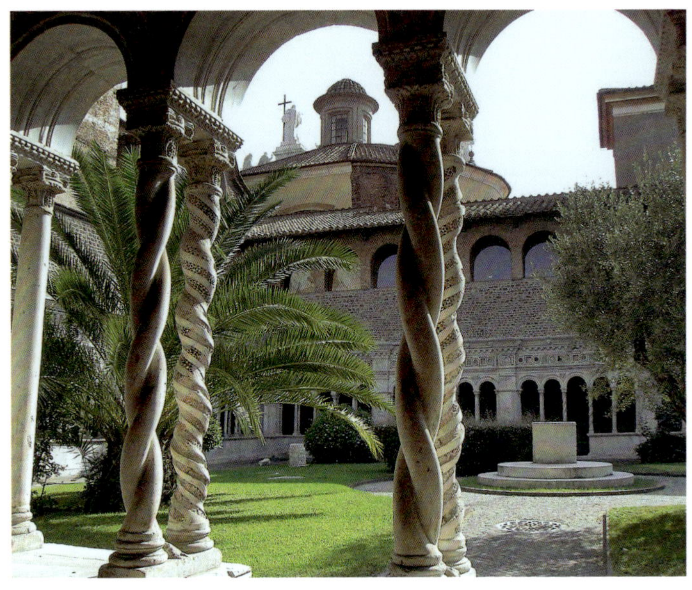

Abb. 17 San Giovanni in Laterano, Kreuzgang mit Kosmati-Mosaiken, Rom, ca. 1200
Fig. 17 San Giovanni in Laterano, Cloister with Cosmatesque decoration, Rome, c. 1200

verwendeten enormen Steinblöcke, den Aufwand und die finanziellen Mitteln, die in diese Gebäude investiert wurden, betonten.[53] Doch obwohl sie zweifellos von den Bauwerken beeindruckt waren, die wir als typisch für die römische Antike erachten, bevorzugten sie die frühchristlichen und mittelalterlichen Bauten, die aus ihrer Sicht ja genauso antik waren. Wenn wir also beim Versuch, die Inspiration der Renaissance durch das alte Rom zu rekonstruieren, nur Zeugnisse des Interesses an antik-römischen Gebäuden berücksichtigen und die bewundernden Beschreibungen der mittelalterlichen Bausubstanz übergehen, weil sie nicht unseren Erwartungen entsprechen, erhalten wir ein verzerrtes Bild von der umfassenden Auseinandersetzung mit der Vergangenheit im 15. Jahrhundert. Ähnlich verhält es sich, wenn

commented on the ancient Roman ruins with awe, focusing on their monumentality and greatness and particularly on the enormous blocks of stone employed in their construction, and they were impressed by the investment evident in these buildings in terms of both labour and funding.[52] But the examples they found most pleasing were the early Christian and medieval ones, which to them, of course, were 'antique' as well. If, in our aim to map inspiration from ancient Rome onto the fifteenth century, we only account for testimonies showing an interest in buildings from antiquity – leaving out the admiring descriptions of medieval material because they do not fit our expectations – we distort the scope of that century's engagement with the past. Similarly, if we explain away the praise of the early Christian and medieval buildings as resulting from a conviction that these were ancient Roman temples, we disregard that the people of the time actually appreciated these structures. It would potentially be more productive to acknowledge that they favoured these buildings because their style represented an adequate ideal, notably more so than unequivocally ancient buildings in Rome such as the Pantheon or the Colosseum.

The drawings made by artists and architects in the fifteenth century confirm the pattern emerging from Giovanni Rucellai's diary, showcasing a decisive centre of gravity around post-classical architecture. Not much is preserved from the first half of the century, the period when Brunelleschi supposedly studied in Rome.[53] Paper is, of course, a fragile material, and in the early fifteenth century – when every sheet of paper was handmade individually – it was still not a commodity that was readily at hand for drawing. But from the tendencies that become apparent when we analyse the existing drawings, it seems unlikely that systematic study of classical Roman architecture existed as a practice at the time – regardless of whether drawings have survived or not.

wir das Lob der frühchristlichen und mittelalterlichen Bauten damit erklären, dass diese als ehemalige antik-römische Tempel betrachtet wurden, und dabei ignorieren, was die Menschen tatsächlich an ihnen schätzten. Wäre es nicht produktiver anzuerkennen, dass sie diese Gebäude bevorzugten, weil ihr Stil ein geeignetes Ideal repräsentierte, und zwar offenbar in größerem Ausmaß als zweifelsfrei antike Bauwerke in Rom wie das Pantheon oder das Kolosseum?

Die Zeichnungen, die von Künstlern und Architekten im 15. Jahrhundert angefertigt wurden, bestätigen das Bild – das sich auch aus dem Tagebuch Giovanni Rucellais ergibt – von einer Vorliebe für nachantike Architektur. Nur wenig ist aus der ersten Hälfte des 15. Jahrhunderts erhalten, der Zeit also, in der Brunelleschi in Rom studiert haben soll.[54] Abgesehen von seiner Fragilität war Papier im 15. Jahrhundert noch kein gängiges Material, das man zum Zeichnen immer zur Hand hatte; jedes Blatt musste einzeln von Hand hergestellt werden. Bei der Analyse der vorhandenen Zeichnungen, zeigen sich einige Tendenzen, die es als unwahrscheinlich erscheinen lassen, dass zu dieser Zeit systematische Studien der klassischen römischen Architektur durchgeführt worden sind.

Die frühesten erhaltenen Zeichnungen stammen aus den 1420er und 1430er Jahren und den darauffolgenden Jahrzehnten und werden Künstlern wie Gentile da Fabriano, Pisanello (Abb. 18), Jacopo Bellini und Benozzo Gozzoli zugeschrieben. Künstler also, die wir hauptsächlich mit der Malerei in Verbindung bringen und nicht Architekten, obwohl die strikte Trennung von Malerei und Architektur natürlich der Moderne zuzurechnen ist. Die Zeichnungen zeigen keine ganzen Gebäude, sondern skulpturale und dekorative Details. Wenn Brunelleschi, der ja auch Bildhauer war, in Rom tatsächlich Zeichnungen anfertigte, dann wäre es naheliegend, dass diese bildhauerischen Details zeigten. Dies würde Manettis etwas kryptische Bemerkung erhellen, dass

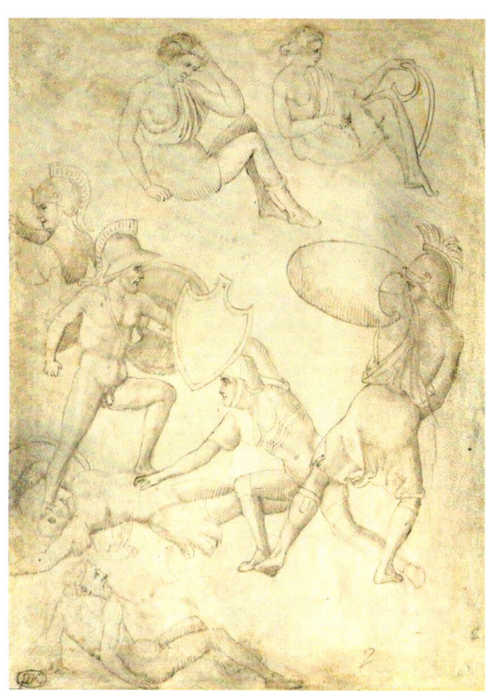

Abb. 18 Pisanello, Figuren eines antik-römischen Sarkophages (Kriegerinnen, die um den Leichnam einer Amazone kämpfen und zwei sitzende Amazonen), ca. 1431–1432, Tinte auf Pergament, 22,3 × 26,7 cm, Rotterdam, Museum Boijmans-van Beuningen

Fig. 18 Pisanello, Drawing of figures from ancient Roman sarcophagus (Warriors Fighting over the Corpse of an Amazon and Two Seated Amazons), c. 1431–1432, Pen and ink and wash on parchment, 22,3 × 26,7 cm, Rotterdam, Museum Boijmans-van Beuningen

The earliest drawings that are preserved date back to the 1420s and the subsequent decades and are attributed to artists we mainly associate with pictorial art – such as Gentile da Fabriano, Pisanello (Fig. 18), Jacopo Bellini, and Benozzo Gozzoli – rather than to architects, although one must bear in mind that any strict segregation of painters from architects belongs to the modern period. The drawings feature sculptural and decorative details, not entire buildings. If

Brunelleschi die Bildhauerei studierte, um die Prinzipien und Manier der antiken Bauweise zu verstehen.[55] Wenn Brunelleschi das Ziel verfolgte, die Bildhauerei zu studieren, würde dies auch Manettis Aussage, Donatello habe nie erkannt, dass Brunelleschi antike Architektur studierte, erklären; eine kuriose Bemerkung, wenn man bedenkt, dass Manetti an anderer Stelle behauptet, die beiden hätten antike Gebäude vermessen und sogar Ausgrabungen durchführen lassen.[56] Die Abneigung des 15. Jahrhunderts gegen eine übermäßig kräftige, körperlich-materielle Architektursprache, die sich im Fehlen von Zeichnungen großer Architekturen zeigt, findet ihre Parallele in der Vermeidung der Darstellung monumentaler hellenistisch-römischer Skulpturen. Die Künstler zeichneten nicht die körperbetonten, dynamischen, freistehenden Skulpturen der Antike, sondern konzentrierten sich auf Kleinformatiges wie Sarkophagreliefs, die aufgrund ihrer Zweidimensionalität filigraner sind und relativ abstrakt bleiben. Ein Beispiel für den Umgang mit antiker Skulptur ist die um 1500 datierte früheste bekannte Zeichnung des Belvedere-Torsos, deren wahrscheinlicher Autor Amico Aspertini die muskulöse männliche Figur in eine schlanke, gotische Form übersetzte (Abb. 19).

Erst in den letzten Jahrzehnten des 15. Jahrhunderts begannen Künstler, die wir mit ihrer architektonischen Praxis in Verbindung bringen, wie Francesco di Giorgio oder Giuliano da Sangallo, Zeichnungen anzufertigen, die ganze Gebäude darstellen (Abb. 16).[57] Entsprechend den, in den schriftlichen Quellen belegten Interessen, zeigen die meisten Architekturzeichnungen des späten 15. Jahrhunderts nachklassische Bauten, die sich auf die dekorativen, die Körperlichkeit auflösenden Elemente konzentrieren – wie etwa die Mosaike in Santa Costanza – oder sie zeigen plastische Reliefs und Kapitelle. Wie Tilman Buddensieg in einer Analyse der Einstellungen zur antiken Architektur im 15. und 16. Jahrhundert (1971)

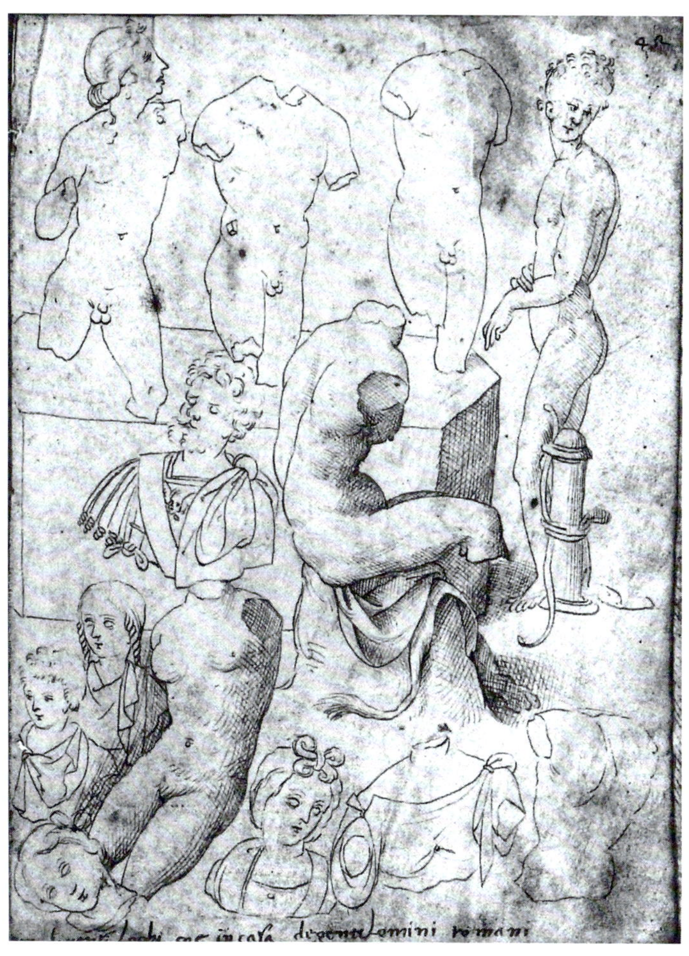

Abb. 19 Amico Aspertini, Studienblatt mit antiken Skulpturen, zentral der Torso Belvedere, ca. 1500–1503, in: *Codex Wolfegg*, Wolfegg, Fürstliche Kunstsammlungen, Fol. 42r

Fig. 19 Amico Aspertini, Drawing of ancient sculpture, with the Belvedere Torso in the center, c. 1500–1503, in: *Codex Wolfegg*, Wolfegg, Fürstliche Kunstsammlungen, fol. 42r

Brunelleschi, who incidentally was a sculptor as well, actually did make drawings in Rome, we may presume that they would have featured such sculptural details. In fact, this

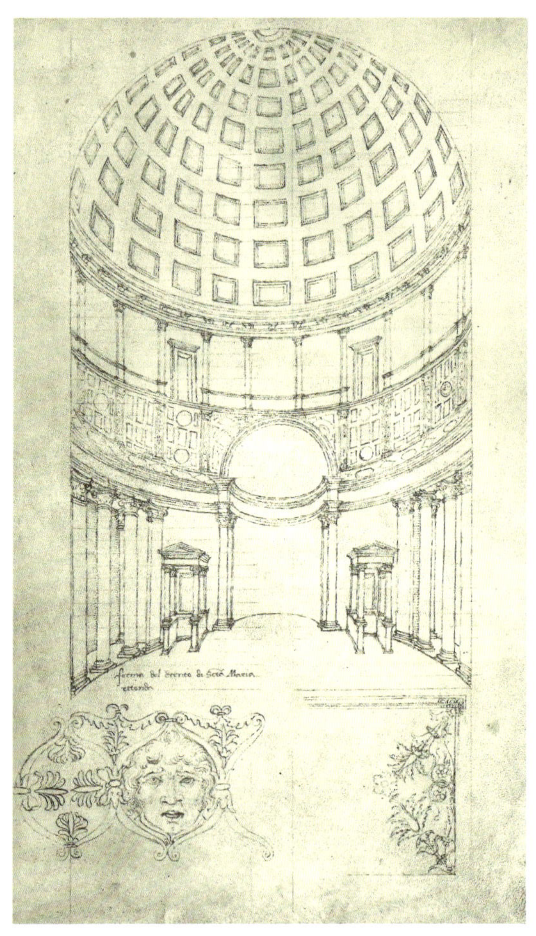

Abb. 20 Francesco di Giorgio, Innenansicht des Pantheons, in: *Codex Saluzziano* 148, Fol. 80r, um 1485, Turin, Biblioteca Reale
Fig. 20 Francesco di Giorgio, Interior of the Pantheon, in: *Codex Saluzziano* 148, fol. 80r, mid 1480s., Turin, Biblioteca Reale

zeigt, tendierte Francesco di Giorgio dazu, die antiken Gebäude zu gotisieren, indem er sie schlanker machte und ihre Vertikalität betonte.[58] Ein Beispiel dafür ist seine Zeichnung des Innenraums des Pantheons, die die antik-römische Struktur durch Einfügung einer Art Mezzanin unter der Kuppel

would clarify Manetti's somewhat obscure remark that Brunelleschi had studied sculpture as a way to understand the principles and manners of the antique way of building.[54] It would also explain Manetti's statement that Donatello never realized that Brunelleschi had studied ancient architecture, which is curious considering Manetti's claim that the two of them measured ancient buildings and even undertook excavations together.[55]

The fifteenth-century aversion to the powerful and materially substantive in architecture, which is witnessed by the lack of drawings of large-scale structures, finds a parallel in the artists' avoidance of representing grand, Hellenistic-Roman sculpture. Indeed, they did not draw the corporeally most emphatic and dynamic free-standing sculpture from antiquity but rather concentrated on models such as sarcophagi reliefs, which are both smaller in size and relatively abstract due to their two-dimensional format. An example is the earliest known drawing of the Belvedere torso, dated to around 1500 and attributed to Amico Aspertini, who translated the muscular male figure into a slender, Gothic form (Fig. 19).

Accordingly, it was not until the last decades of the fifteenth century that artists we associate with a practice as architects, such as Francesco di Giorgio or Giuliano da Sangallo, began to produce drawings representing entire buildings (Fig. 16).[56] Corresponding to the interest displayed in the written sources, the majority of the late fifteenth-century drawings of architecture depict either post-classical buildings or sculptural reliefs and capitals, or else they concentrate on the decorative, corporeality-dissolving elements of a building, like the mosaics in Santa Costanza. As once demonstrated by Tilman Buddensieg in an analysis of fifteenth- and sixteenth-century attitudes to ancient architecture (1971), Francesco di Giorgio tended to 'Gothicize' the ancient buildings, making them slenderer and accentuating

zur Verstärkung der Vertikalität sozusagen korrigiert (Abb. 20). Indem Francesco di Giorgio das geometrische Grundprinzip des antiken Tempels – Durchmesser gleich Höhe – durchbrach, konnte er eine leichtere Version des Gebäudes imaginieren.

In seiner Analyse der Zeichnungen interpretiert Buddensieg solche Modifikationen als Kritik an den antik-römischen Vorbildern.[59] Durch seine Zeichnungen verbesserte Francesco di Giorgio die antik-römischen Bauten, indem er sie in Versionen übersetzte, die gotischer, weniger aufdringlich körperlich und damit näher an seiner eigenen künstlerischen Sprache des 15. Jahrhunderts waren. Buddensieg zeigt, dass solche Transformationen der antiken Architektur in der Zeichnung um 1500 typisch waren. Die Architekten ordneten und adjustierten die Grundrisse der antiken Bauten und verliehen den einzelnen Bauteilen eine geometrische Genauigkeit und Symmetrie, die den alten Römern fremd war.[60] Wie Buddensieg überzeugend darlegt, beruhte diese kritische Anpassung der antiken Vorbilder auf einer neuen architektonischen Systematisierung, die sich erst in der Gotik richtig durchgesetzt hatte.

Neue Paradigmen der Genauigkeit und Ordnung

Obwohl sowohl die Archäologie als auch die Kunstgeschichte erst ab dem 19. Jahrhundert systematisiert und akademisiert wurden, zeichnete sich in den ersten Jahrzehnten des 16. Jahrhunderts ein Umbruch im Umgang mit antiker Architektur ab, der zu Herangehensweisen führte, die mit den modernen archäologischen und kunsthistorischen Methoden vergleichbar sind. Ein bedeutender Zeuge dieser Neuerungen des 16. Jahrhunderts ist Raffael, der als päpstlicher Aufseher über die römischen Antiken überdurchschnittlich gut mit der

their verticality.[57] One example is his drawing of the interior of the Pantheon, where he corrected the ancient Roman structure by inserting a kind of mezzanine below the dome and thereby heightened its verticality (Fig. 20). By disrupting the basic geometry of the ancient Roman temple, in which the diameter of the building is equal to its height, he achieved a lighter version of the building.

In his analysis of Francesco di Giorgio's drawings, Buddensieg deemed such modifications a 'criticism' of the ancient Roman models.[58] The architect improved the ancient buildings by translating them into versions that were more Gothic, less obtrusively corporeal, and thus closer to his own fifteenth-century artistic idiom. Buddensieg demonstrated that such revisions of the ancient Roman architecture in drawing were typical around 1500. Architects adjusted the floor plans of the ancient buildings, ordering their components via a geometric accuracy and symmetry that had been foreign to the ancient Romans.[59] As convincingly argued by Buddensieg, this critical reworking of the ancient models was based on a new inclination, from the Gothic period on, towards systematization.

New Paradigms of Accuracy and Order

Although archaeology and art history did not become systematized and academic until the nineteenth century, a breakthrough in the observation of ancient architecture, moving towards approaches more in line with modern archaeological and art-historical methods, began to take shape in the first decades of the sixteenth century. A major testimony to these innovations of the sixteenth century is found in Raphael, whose employment as administrator of the antiquities that were being unearthed in Rome and its surrounds involved an

urbanen Struktur Roms vertraut war. Das Ziel der von Raffael beaufsichtigten Vermessungsarbeiten war nicht zuletzt praktischer Natur: Sie lieferten Informationen darüber, wo die Baumeister Material und Spolien für die Wiederverwendung in großen Bauprojekten wie dem neuen Petersdom finden konnten.[61] Wohl um 1519 schrieb Raffael zusammen mit dem Gelehrten Baldassare Castiglione (1478–1529) und dem Epigraphiker Angelo Colocci (1474–1544) einen berühmten Brief, in dem er ein Projekt beschrieb, das angeblich von Papst Leo X. (dem Sohn Lorenzo de' Medicis) in Auftrag gegeben worden war, nämlich eine zeichnerische Rekonstruktion des antiken Roms.[62] Der Brief ist eine wichtige und aufschlussreiche Quelle in der Frage nach dem Antikenbegriff des frühen 16. Jahrhunderts. In unserem Zusammenhang sind besonders jene Argumente von Interesse, die vorgebracht wurden, um das Projekt als realisierbar darzustellen. Raffael und seine Mitautoren waren sichtlich darum bemüht, ihren bedeutenden Empfänger davon zu überzeugen, dass es prinzipiell möglich ist, die antiken Gebäude von den späteren zu unterscheiden:

> [...] weil es eventuell Eurer Heiligkeit so scheinen könnte, als ob das Unterscheiden der antiken Bauwerke von den modernen und der ältesten von den weniger alten schwierig sei [...] meine ich, dass dies mit geringer Mühe möglich ist [...].[63]

Raffael behauptet also nicht bloß, dass die Unterscheidung zwischen den Bauten des antiken Roms, den nachfolgenden Epochen der gotischen Architektur und der zeitgenössischen Architektur kein Problem darstellt, sondern auch, dass er zwischen älteren und jüngeren antiken Bauwerken unterscheiden kann, im Original »li più antichi dalli meno antichi«.[64] Dass es notwendig war, den Papst von der prinzipiellen Durchführbarkeit des Projekts zu überzeugen, zeigt, wie

above-average knowledge of the urban fabric of the city. The objective of this professional role was not least a practical one, mapping where masons could find material and spolia for use in vast building projects like that of the new St Peter's.[60] Presumably around 1519, Raphael co-wrote a famous letter with the learned Baldassare Castiglione and the epigraphist Angelo Colocci, describing a project allegedly ordered by Pope Leo X (the son of Lorenzo de' Medici), namely a reconstruction in drawing of ancient Rome.[61] The letter is an important, eye-opening source for the whole question of the period's concept of antiquity. In our context, it is particularly interesting to read the arguments justifying the feasibility of the project in the first place. Raphael and his co-authors had to make efforts to convince their distinguished reader that it was possible to discern the ancient buildings from the later ones. He asserted that:

> since telling the difference between ancient and modern buildings, or between those more ancient and less ancient, might seem to some to be difficult, and so as not to leave any doubt whatsoever in the mind of someone who wishes to acquire this ability to discriminate, I say that this can be done with very little effort.[62]

Raphael not only claimed that there were no problems involved in distinguishing among the buildings of ancient Rome, of the Gothic period, and of his own present, but he even asserted that he could differentiate the "more ancient" from the "less ancient", "li più antichi dalli meno antichi".[63] This attempt to make the project appear easy is quite touching. The fact that it was necessary at all to convince the pope of its feasibility implies the difficulty entailed in approaching the entanglement of architectural structures from various historical periods and in visually dissecting their various

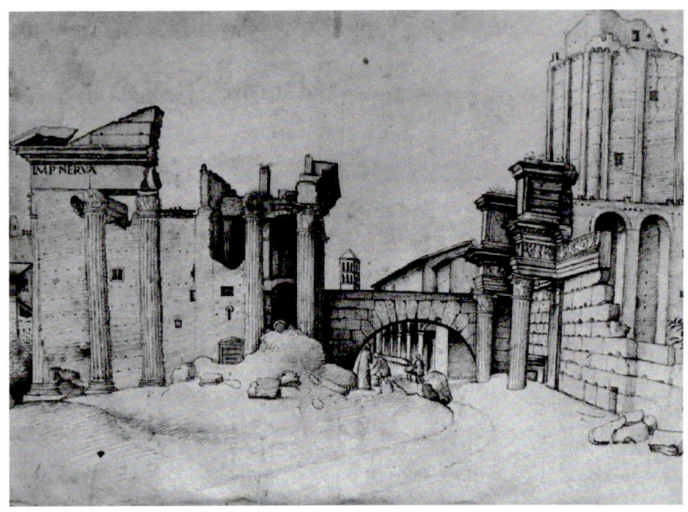

Abb. 21 Romansicht mit dem Nerva-Forum, die die Überbauung von
antik-römischer Architektur mit mittelalterlichen Gebäuden zeigt, ca. 1500,
in: *Codex Escurialensis*, Madrid, Real Biblioteca del Monasterio de
San Lorenzo de El Escorial, Fol. 57v
Fig. 21 Prospect of Rome (Forum of Nerva), with its remains of ancient
Roman architecture rebuilt and supplemented with new buildings in the
medieval period, c. 1500, in: *Codex Escurialensis*, Real Biblioteca del
Monasterio de San Lorenzo de El Escorial, fol. 57v

schwierig es damals war, sich dem Durcheinander architektonischer Strukturen verschiedener historischer Epochen zu
nähern, die Schichten visuell zu differenzieren und zu ent-
scheiden, welche davon tatsächlich dem antiken Rom entstammten. Die antiken Bauwerke waren überbaut, um Spolien beraubt und teilweise meterhoch von Schutt und Erde
bedeckt, die sich im Laufe der Jahrhunderte angesammelt
hatten (Abb. 21). Die Untersuchung der antiken römischen
Überreste war daher in jeder Hinsicht sehr herausfordernd.

Trotz Raffaels selbstbewusster Behauptungen führten
seine stilistischen Analysen zur dürftigen Konklusion, dass
die Architektur der römischen Antike perfekt war und dass

layers to determine which ones derived from ancient Rome. The ancient structures were overbuilt, spoliated, and partly covered by many meters of dirt, which had accumulated through the centuries (Fig. 21). This made investigation of the ancient Roman remains inaccessible in a very literal way.

But despite Raphael's confident assertions, his stylistic analyses consisted simply of observing that the architecture of Roman antiquity was perfect and that the ancient patrons had spent enormous amounts of money and great effort on building. Gothic architecture, on the other hand, was barbarous; and the new buildings of the city were very easy to detect as well, because they were new: "Li edifici adunqua moderni sono notissimi [...] per esser novi".[64] This circularity of argument clearly exposes the limited tools of stylistic designation and analysis that were available even to Raphael and his learned companions. His historical survey is also revealing, in that he defined the medieval period as lasting for about a hundred years: He divided the history of architecture into three periods. The first is the good, antique style, what he calls the manner of those "good ancients", "quelli buoni antichi"; it lasted until its destruction by the barbarian invasions, which by modern metrics took place in the early fifth century when Rome was invaded by Goths for the first time.[65] Then followed a decline beginning with the regime of the Goths, which by modern standards would mean the sixth century, and extending one hundred years, through the seventh century.[66] Finally, the third period – or *maniera* (manner), as he calls it – is the modern one, stretching from the seventh century to Raphael's own time.[67]

It is not surprising that Panofsky struggled to accept Raphael's description of the Middle Ages as lasting only a hundred years. In a footnote, Panofsky stated that: "The phrase 'a hundred years thereafter' (*é ancora cento anni d'appoi*) would seem to indicate an indefinite period of considerable length (as we

die antiken Bauherren enorme Geldbeträge und große Anstrengungen aufgewandt hatten. Die gotische Architektur wurde hingegen als barbarisch abgewertet und die neueren Gebäude der Stadt konnten erstaunlich leicht identifiziert werden, einfach weil sie neu waren: »Li edifici adunqua moderni sono notissimi [...] per esser novi«.[65] Diese zirkuläre Argumentation zeigt deutlich auf, dass die stilistischen Analyseinstrumente und das Vokabular, die Raffael und seinen gelehrten Kollegen zur Verfügung standen, äußerst begrenzt waren. Auch ein im Brief gegebener historischer Überblick ist aufschlussreich, denn er definiert das Mittelalter als eine Zeitspanne von etwa hundert Jahren. Raffael unterteilt die Geschichte der Architektur in drei Perioden: Die erste entspricht dem guten, antiken Stil – er bezeichnet ihn als die Manier jener guten Alten, »quelli buoni antichi« –, der bis zur Zerstörung durch gotische Invasionen gepflegt wurde, womit sich Raffael wohl auf die Eroberung Roms durch die Goten im frühen 5. Jahrhundert bezieht.[66] Darauf folgte aus Raffaels Sicht ein Niedergang, der mit der gotischen Herrschaft begann und hundert Jahre andauern sollte, also vom 6. bis ins 7. Jahrhundert.[67] Die dritte Periode oder Manier, die moderne Periode, erstreckte sich von da an bis in seine eigene Zeit.[68] Es ist nicht verwunderlich, dass Panofsky große Schwierigkeiten damit hatte, Raffaels Beschreibung des Mittelalters als eine hundertjährige Periode zu akzeptieren. In einer Fußnote behauptet er:

> The phrase ›a hundred years thereafter‹ (*é ancora cento anni d'appoi*) would seem to indicate an indefinite period of considerable length (as we say, »This will take a hundred times longer«) rather than just a century.[69]

Obwohl sich Panofsky der schwammigen Bedeutung von *antico* bewusst war, konnte er Raffaels Auffassung, dass das

say, 'This will take a hundred times longer') rather than just a century".[68] Despite Panofsky's awareness of the muddy meaning of *antico*, he could not reconcile Raphael's concept of the one-century-long Middle Ages with his own expectations that this major High Renaissance artist would have possessed a clear historical consciousness. What seemed to be an astonishing ignorance on Raphael's part did not match the picture Panofsky was assembling of the period, namely as having breathed life into a new historical consciousness. As it did not make sense to Panofsky that Raphael's grasp of history had been so imprecise, he ignored it by suggesting that by "a hundred years" the artist had actually meant something else.

However, there is no evidence that Raphael did not simply mean what he wrote. The artist's phrasing rather indicates that his and his co-authors' notion of periodization differed from the one that has since been naturalized by modern art history. The era immediately following the invasion by the Goths was conflated with the subsequent medieval era, which, to Raphael, had been dominated by a Gothic manner. The passage in the letter is important because it reveals Raphael's alternative way of delimiting the epochs of antiquity and the Middle Ages, compared to our modern periodization.

In addition to displaying Raphael's somewhat foggy view of art history, the letter is remarkable because, in it, the artist meticulously described the actual methods they were using in their survey.[69] His elaborate instructions on how to map and draw architecture expose that the elite of the time, and even the culturally sophisticated Pope Leo X, were unaccustomed to the modern conventions of systematic surveys. Raphael articulated their intention to represent the buildings in terms of plan as well as elevation, which he called the 'exterior wall', and section, which he called the 'interior wall'.[70] He moreover added perspective views (orthogonal projections), as a drawing format that facilitated the visualization of a building.[71]

Mittelalter nur hundert Jahre dauerte, nicht mit seiner Erwartung an diesen bedeutenden Künstler der Hochrenaissance in Einklang bringen, ein klares Geschichtsbewusstsein besessen zu haben. Was als erstaunliche Ignoranz Raffaels erscheinen musste, passt schlecht in das Bild einer vom neuen Geschichtsbewusstsein beseelten Epoche, das Panofsky zeichnete. Da es für Panofsky unvorstellbar war, dass Raffaels Überblick über die Vergangenheit so ungenau gewesen sein konnte, ignorierte er die Evidenz und behauptete, dass Raffael zwar hundert Jahre schrieb, aber eigentlich etwas anderes gemeint habe.

Nichts deutet jedoch darauf hin, dass Raffael nicht meinte, was er schrieb. Seine Formulierungen zeigen, dass er und seine Mitautoren nicht mit der Periodisierung arbeiteten, die von der modernen Kunstgeschichte kodifiziert wurde. Die Zeit nach der gotischen Invasion wurde mit dem nachfolgenden Mittelalter vermengt, das aus Raffaels Sicht von der gotischen Manier dominiert wurde. Diese Passage in Raffaels Brief ist wichtig, weil sie Raffaels völlig anderen Zugang zur Abgrenzung der Perioden der Antike und des Mittelalters im Vergleich zu unserer modernen Periodisierung aufzeigt.

Neben seinem etwas unscharfen kunsthistorischen Überblick ist Raffaels Brief auch deshalb bemerkenswert, weil er die Methoden, die sie bei ihrer Vermessung anwandten, akribisch beschreibt.[70] Seine ausführlichen Anweisungen zum Vermessen und Zeichnen von Architektur zeigen, dass die damalige Elite und sogar der kunstsinnige Papst Leo X. mit den neuesten Konventionen der systematischen Vermessung nicht vertraut waren. Raffael formulierte das Vorhaben, die Gebäude durch Grundriss, Aufriss, den er »Außenwand« nannte, und Schnitt, als »Innenwand« bezeichnet, zu repräsentieren.[71] Darüber hinaus fügte er perspektivische Ansichten (orthogonale Projektionen) hinzu, um die Visualisierung von Gebäuden zu erleichtern.[72] Die bloße Tatsache, dass er

The mere fact that he needed to laboriously describe what an architectural plan was testifies to the novelty of this method of drawing.[72] Indeed, if the formats of architectural drawing had been common knowledge to the pope and his entourage, it would not have been necessary for Raphael to include such a description in his letter. But in fact, the practice of recording buildings in this systematic, objective manner had only just begun to manifest itself (Fig. 16). Some architectural drawings dating to the last decades of the fifteenth century feature plans in the modern sense, though they do not yet delineate the buildings more than schematically. In certain cases, the new concept of an architectural plan as a horizontal cross-section of the building at ground level was combined with older visualization formats, as in the treatise by Filarete (Fig. 22).[73] In the drawings preceding the development of the modern formats, architects only represented interiors, but not proper sections (Fig. 20). Like a plan, a section is a cut-through – this time, vertically oriented – of a building. Both involve accurate representations of the thickness of the walls, and their intelligibility is enhanced by the convention of representing the materiality and solidity of the wall by shading it in grey. In Francesco di Giorgio's drawing of Santa Costanza, we see one of the earliest representations of this modern concept of the section, however, still only indicated by its contour (Fig. 16). It is in slightly later drawings by Leonardo da Vinci and Giuliano da Sangallo that we encounter the first sections in the modern sense, where the cut-through of the wall and its materiality is indicated (Fig. 23).

In addition to bearing witness to the novelty of recording architecture in these formats of drawing in the early sixteenth century, the letter reveals the emphasis Raphael placed on the precision required in architectural drawing. He wrote, for instance, that the discipline of architectural drawing "demands complete accuracy of measurements and lines drawn

detailliert erklären musste, was ein architektonischer Plan ist, zeugt von der Neuartigkeit dieser Methode.[73] Wären dem Papst und seinem Gefolge diese Typen architektonischer Zeichnungen bekannt gewesen, hätte Raffael ihre Beschreibung nicht in seinen Brief aufnehmen müssen. Tatsächlich stand die Praxis, Gebäude auf diese systematische, objektive Weise zu dokumentieren, gerade am Anfang (Abb. 16). Architekturzeichnungen der letzten Jahrzehnte des 15. Jahrhunderts sind die ersten, die Pläne im modernen Sinne umfassen, auch wenn die Gebäude noch höchst schematisch umrissen sind. Mitunter wurde das moderne Konzept eines Architekturplans als horizontaler Schnitt durch das Gebäude auf Bodenhöhe mit älteren Darstellungsformen kombiniert, etwa im Traktat von Filarete (Abb. 22).[74] In den Zeichnungen, die der Entwicklung der modernen Darstellungskonventionen vorausgingen, repräsentierten die Architekten nur Innenräume, aber nicht als richtige Schnitte (Abb. 20). Beim horizontalen Plan und beim vertikalen Schnitt wird die Dicke der Wände genau repräsentiert, und ihre Lesbarkeit wird durch die Konvention erhöht, die Materialität und Solidität der Wand durch graue Schattierungen anzuzeigen. In Francesco di Giorgios Zeichnung von Santa Costanza sehen wir eines der frühesten Beispiele für dieses neue Konzept des Schnitts, der allerdings nur durch Konturen angedeutet ist (Abb. 16). In den etwas späteren Zeichnungen Leonardo da Vincis und Giuliano da Sangallos finden wir erstmals Schnitte im modernen Sinne, in denen der Schnitt durch die Wand und ihre Materialität angezeigt werden (Abb. 23).

Der Brief zeugt nicht nur davon, dass es zu Beginn des 16. Jahrhundert noch neu und ungewohnt war, Architektur durch diese Arten von Zeichnungen zu repräsentieren, sondern Raffael sah sich auch dazu veranlasst, die für die Architekturzeichnung erforderliche Präzision zu betonen. Er stellte beispielsweise fest, dass die Disziplin des Architektur-

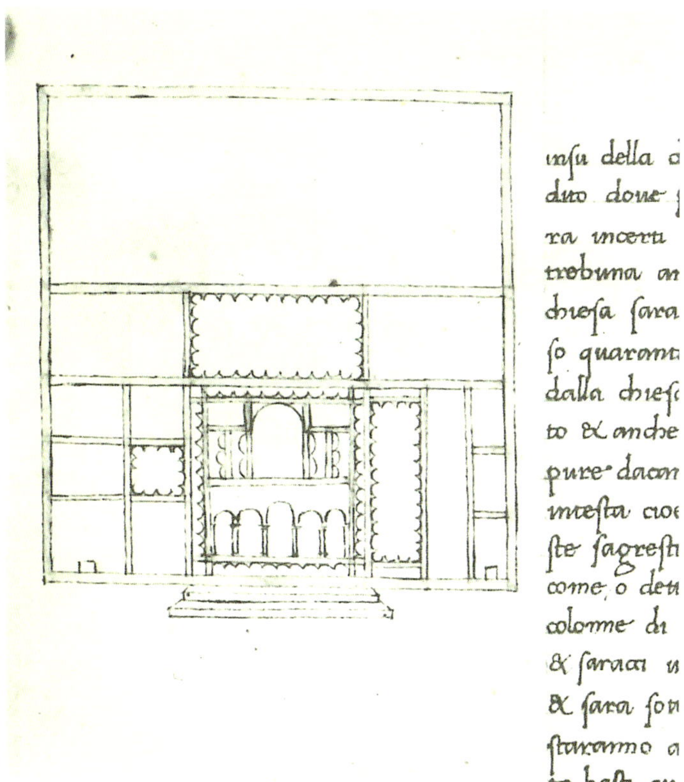

Abb. 22 Filarete, Plan, in: Ders., *Libro Architettonico*, um 1465, in: *Codex Magliabechiano* II.I.140, Florenz, Biblioteca Nazionale, Fol. 78v (Detail)
Fig. 22 Plan from Filarete's *Libro Architettonico*, mid 1460s., in: *Codex Magliabechiano* II.I.140, Florence, Biblioteca Nazionale, fol. 78v (detail)

parallel, not lines that appear to be parallel but that are not so".[74] Perhaps his remarks here about the accurate drawing of parallel lines was intended as a means of distinguishing this format from painterly practices, but the emphasis on exactness is nevertheless pivotal. Already at the beginning of his letter, he asserted that the intention was to draw the surviving buildings "exactly as they were, without error, using true principles", thereby reconstructing the ruins to their original,

zeichnens größte Genauigkeit der Messungen und der parallel gezeichneten Linien verlange, die »tatsächlich vollkommen sind, nicht jene, die als solche nur dem Auge erscheinen, es aber nicht sind«.[75] Womöglich war seine Bemerkung über das genaue Zeichnen paralleler Linien auch als bewusste Abgrenzung zu malerischen Praktiken gedacht; die Betonung der Exaktheit ist jedenfalls von zentraler Bedeutung. Schon zu Beginn des Briefes bekräftigte er, dass es darum gehe, die erhaltenen Gebäude so zu zeichnen, »dass sie mit richtiger Beweisführung unfehlbar in denjenigen Zustand zurückgeführt werden können, in dem sie sich befanden«, also eine Rekonstruktion der Ruinen, die die Gebäude in ihrem ursprünglichen, unversehrten Zustand erscheinen lässt.[76] Aus dem Brief geht deutlich hervor, dass der systematische Ansatz an sich neuartig war und für die Adressaten schwer verständlich gewesen sein musste. Er zeugt von der Neuartigkeit objektiver und geometrisch einheitlicher Architekturdarstellungen um 1520.

In seiner brillanten Darstellung der mittelalterlichen Konzeption von Architekturkopie »Introduction to an ›Iconography of Mediaeval Architecture‹« von 1942 stellte Richard Krautheimer mit Aussagen wie der folgenden fest, dass geometrische Präzision für die Vorstellungswelt der mittelalterlichen Architekten irrelevant war: »It could almost be said that to mediaeval eyes anything which had more than four sides was approximately a circle«.[77] Ein gutes Beispiel hierfür ist Isidor von Sevilla, der bereits im 7. Jahrhundert in seinen einflussreichen enzyklopädischen *Etymologiae* ein Quadrat als aus vier geraden Linien bestehend definiert. Eine moderne Definition würde natürlich betonen, dass diese Linien gleich lang sein und die Winkel 90° betragen müssen. Die Beobachtungen Krautheimers lassen sich bis in die römische Antike zurückverfolgen; etwa zur Beschreibung der Pyramiden bei Plinius d. Ä.: »Each of the four sides has an equal

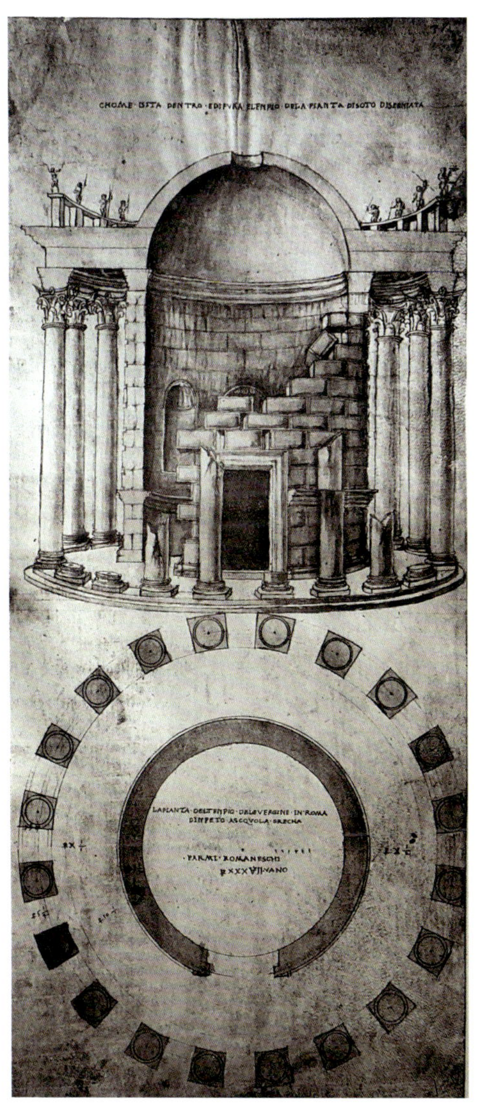

Abb. 23 Giuliano da Sangallo, Schnitte (in Kombination mit Ansichten von Ruinen) und Pläne, ca. 1500, in: *Codice Vaticano Barberiniano Latino 4424*, Vatikanstadt, Biblioteca Apostolica Vaticana, Fol. 37r (Detail)
Fig. 23 Giuliano da Sangallo, Sections (combined with ruinous prospects) and plans, c. 1500, in: *Codice Vaticano Barberiniano Latino 4424*, Vatican City, Biblioteca Apostolica Vaticana, fol. 37r (detail)

measurement from corner to corner of 783 feet; the height from ground-level to the pinnacle amounts to 725 feet, while the circumference of the pinnacle is 16 ½ feet.«[78] Diese Informationen würden einem modernen Menschen, der nicht bereits weiß, wie eine Pyramide aussieht, durchaus einige Anstrengung abverlangen, um sich den Gebäudetyp vorstellen zu können. Trotz Euklids Beschreibung der geometrischen Grundfiguren wurde die systematische Anwendung solcher Definitionen erst im 18. Jahrhundert gebräuchlich.[79] Wenn Leon Battista Alberti in *De re aedificatoria*, das er einige Jahrzehnte vor der posthumen Veröffentlichung 1485 verfasst hatte, feststellt: »Bei viereckigen Grundflächen wird der Fehler der Missgestalt dann am größten sein, wenn nicht alle Winkel rechte sind« und Raffael fordert, parallele Linien so zu zeichnen, dass sie tatsächlich parallel sind, wollten sie zweifellos die von Krautheimer beschriebenen Konvention ungefährer Annäherung durchbrechen.[80] Raffaels Vorgaben zeigen, dass geometrische Präzision zu Beginn des 16. Jahrhunderts noch keine selbstverständliche Bedingung der Architekturzeichnung war. Der allgemeine Ordnungsdrang in der Architektur beschleunigte sich jedoch gegen 1500, was sich zum Beispiel am innovativen Konzept der Säulenordnungen, also der Festlegung einer systematischen ›Ordnung‹ der verschiedenen Säulen- und Gesimsarten und ihrer Proportionen, zeigt.[81] Als Raffael seinen Brief an Papst Leo X. verfasste, war die Anwendung des Begriffs ›Ordnung‹ auf das System der Säulen und Kapitelle noch neu.[82] Der dem Begriff innewohnende Ordnungsprozess spiegelt die zeittypische Neigung zur Systematisierung wider.

Die Aufmerksamkeit für Kapitelle und Säulen kommt in der zweiten Hälfte des 15. Jahrhunderts auf (Abb. 24).[83] Vitruv, die unangefochtene Autorität der antiken römischen Architektur, beschreibt zwar verschiedene Arten von Kapitellen, nicht aber ›Ordnungen‹, zudem war und ist seine

intact state.[75] Throughout the letter, it is evident that a systematic approach was, in itself, new to the intended readers and thus potentially difficult to understand. The letter testifies to the novelty of objective and geometrically unequivocal representations of architecture in Italy around 1520.

In his brilliant account of the medieval concept of the copy in architecture, entitled "Introduction to an 'Iconography of Mediaeval Architecture'" (1942), Richard Krautheimer observed that geometrical precision was not inherent in the mental habits of medieval architects. As Krautheimer put it: "It could almost be said that to mediaeval eyes anything which had more than four sides was approximately a circle".[76] Back in the seventh century, in his influential and encyclopaedic *Etymologies*, Isidore of Seville, for instance, had defined a square as consisting of four straight lines. A modern definition would obviously rather stress that the lines must be equal in length and must intersect at angles of 90 degrees. Krautheimer's observations can be extended back to Roman antiquity. Pliny the Elder described the pyramids in the following way: "Each of the four sides has an equal measurement from corner to corner of 783 feet; the height from ground-level to the pinnacle amounts to 725 feet, while the circumference of the pinnacle is 16 ½ feet".[77] For a modern mind, and assuming no prior knowledge of what a pyramid looks like, visualizing the building-type on the basis of this information demands some effort. Despite Euclid's description of the basic geometric figures, the systematic application of such definitions on an everyday basis did not become common until the eighteenth century.[78] When, in *De re aedificatoria* (published in 1485 though written a couple of decades earlier), Leon Battista Alberti stated that "it is a considerable defect in a four-sided plan if the angles are not exact right angles", and when Raphael called for parallel lines to be rendered in drawing so that they were actually parallel, they

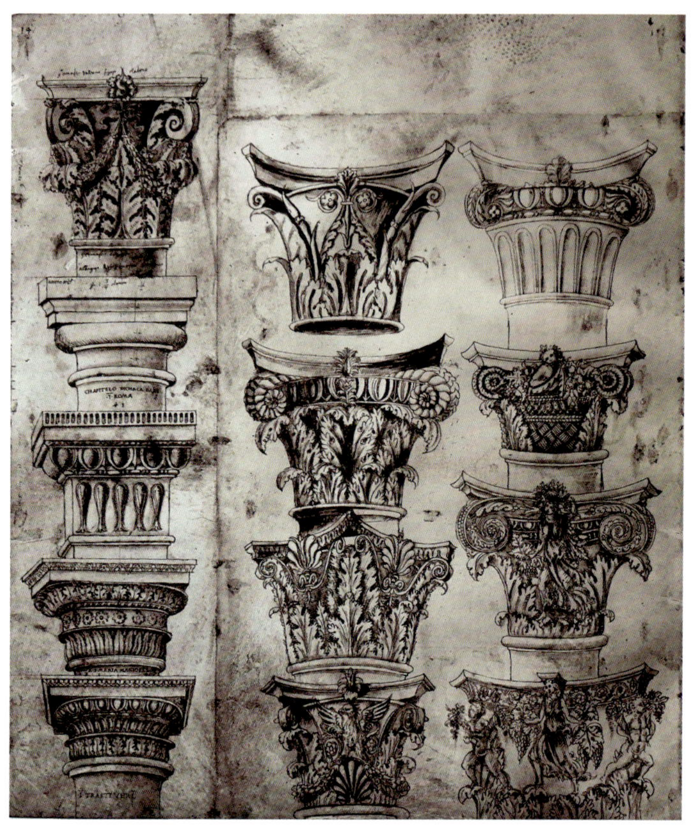

Abb. 24 Giuliano da Sangallo, Verschiedene Kapitelle, ca. 1500, in: *Codice Vaticano Barberiniano Latino 4424*, Vatikanstadt, Biblioteca Apostolica Vaticana, Fol. 14v
Fig. 24 Giuliano da Sangallo, Samples of capitals, c. 1500, in: *Codice Vaticano Barberiniano Latino 4424*, Vatican City, Biblioteca Apostolica Vaticana, fol. 14v

Abhandlung schwer verständlich und nicht illustriert. Die Architekten der zweiten Hälfte des 15. Jahrhunderts waren hingegen bestrebt, genaue Definitionen zu treffen. In diesem Sinne behauptete Manetti, dass Brunelleschi während seiner Jahre in Rom zu Beginn des Jahrhunderts die verschiedenen Arten von klassischen Säulen und Kapitellen studiert und

were objecting to the conventional practice of approximation described by Krautheimer.[79] Raphael's guidelines indicate that, by the early sixteenth century, geometric precision
was still not a self-evident condition of architectural drawing. Yet the overall urge to order the field of architecture accelerated towards 1500, as evident, for instance, in the innovative concept of the orders of columns, of *ordering* the
various types and ornaments of columns and entablatures
and their proportions.[80] At the time of Raphael's letter to
Pope Leo X, the application of the term 'orders' to the system
of columns and capitals was new.[81] The ordering process inherent in the term reflects the predilection for systematizing
that was becoming increasingly pervasive.

An attention to capitals and columns characterized the latter half of the fifteenth century (Fig. 24).[82] The unchallenged
authority on architecture from ancient Rome, Vitruvius, had
only written about different types of capitals, not about 'orders' in general, and, moreover, his treatise was unillustrated
and difficult to read. Architects of the second half of the fifteenth century, by contrast, were eager to arrive at accurate
definitions. In line with this trend, Manetti claimed that
Brunelleschi had studied and learned all about the various
species of classical columns and capitals during his years in
Rome at the beginning of the century.[83] This is not corroborated by the buildings designed by Brunelleschi, which almost
exclusively feature Corinthian capitals.[84] But it attests, once
again, to how Manetti re-attributed endeavours to Brunelleschi
that in fact reflect novel interests of his own day.

An early and major testimony to the preoccupation with
the orders is Leon Battista Alberti's *De re aedificatoria*, begun
c. 1450, the theoretically most informed treatise on architecture of the period. But Filarete and Francesco di Giorgio are
also representative of the preoccupation with capitals and
columns.[85] The topic is similarly recurrent in the drawings of

gemeistert habe.[84] Diese Behauptung kann durch die von Brunelleschi entworfenen Gebäude jedoch nicht bestätigt werden, da er fast ausschließlich korinthische Kapitelle einsetzte.[85] Aber es zeigt einmal mehr, dass Manetti Brunelleschi Interessen und Bemühungen zuschreibt, die seiner eigenen Zeit entstammten.

Ein frühes und wichtiges Zeugnis des Interesses an den Säulenordnungen und der theoretisch fundierteste Architekturtraktat der Zeit ist Leon Battista Albertis *De re aedificatoria,* begonnen um 1450. Aber auch Filarete und Francesco di Giorgio sind wichtige Protagonisten der intensiven Beschäftigung mit Kapitellen und Säulen.[86] Zudem bezeugen die Architekturzeichnungen dieser Zeit, in denen Skizzen von Kapitellen und Basen einen Großteil der erhaltenen Blätter einnehmen, die intensive Auseinandersetzung mit diesem Thema.[87] Zugleich demonstrieren die kunsttheoretischen Überlegungen des 15. Jahrhunderts zu den antiken römischen Ordnungen deutlich die Vagheit Vitruvs; wobei sich die schwere Verständlichkeit seiner Schreibweise durch die Tradierung von Fehlern der mittelalterlichen Kopisten und die unvermeidlichen Unklarheiten des Texts – nicht zuletzt bezüglich der Maßangaben – im Laufe der Jahrhundert noch verstärkt hatte.[88]

Es ist daher nicht verwunderlich, dass Alberti trotz aller Gelehrsamkeit die architektonischen Elemente in seinen Kirchen und Profanbauten anders anwandte als die antiken Römer, auch wenn er in *De re aedificatoria* betonte, wie viel Mühe er in das Studium der Überreste des antiken Roms investiert hatte.[89] Erst zu Beginn des 16. Jahrhunderts begegnen wir in den Bauten Bramantes Säulenordnungen, die gemäß der Systematik ausgeführt und eingesetzt wurden, die für die folgenden Jahrhunderte kanonisiert werden sollte. Die früheste Darstellung in einem gedruckten Buch folgte mit dem ersten Band des architektonischen Traktats

architecture that date to this period, the extant sheets being frequently occupied by sketches of capitals and bases.[86] However, these art-theoretical reflections of the fifteenth century on the ancient Roman orders clearly demonstrate the vagueness of Vitruvius, a characteristic of his original text that had only increased through the ages as a result of medieval scribes' inevitable misunderstandings and corruptions, not least of his indications of measurements.[87]

It is thus no wonder that – despite his erudition, as well as his statement in *De re aedificatoria* of how much effort he had invested in studying the remains of antiquity – Alberti's application of the architectural elements to his churches and secular buildings yielded designs that differed from those of the ancient Romans.[88] It was not until the early sixteenth century, in buildings by Bramante, that we encounter the orders executed and deployed in a form consistent with the system that would be subsequently canonized; and these were illustrated, for the first time in a printed book, in the first volume of Sebastiano Serlio's architectural treatise, published in 1537 (Fig. 25).[89] When Raphael, in his letter to Pope Leo X, offers a thorough presentation of the 'orders', it is clear as well that they were not yet common knowledge.[90] Here again, the letter marks a new shift towards the systematization that would develop further in the sixteenth century.

In line with this, insight into the orders was of major importance to Giorgio Vasari. The impressive account of art and architectural history that he was able to compose in his introduction to the *Vite* displays a conspicuous leap from the vague theoretical and historical approaches to architecture that had been typical of the fifteenth century.[91] The text testifies to the sixteenth century's dramatic accumulation of knowledge, facilitated by the media of books and images following the technical innovation of the printing press. Vasari's absorption with the orders went hand in hand with his

von Sebastiano Serlio von 1537 (Abb. 25).[90] Dass Raffael in seinem Brief an Papst Leo X. eine ausführliche Darstellung der ›Ordnungen‹ bietet, verdeutlicht nicht bloß, dass diese noch nicht allgemein bekannt waren, sondern markiert auch den neuen Zug zur Systematisierung, die sich im 16. Jahrhundert fortsetzen sollte.[91]

Dementsprechend war die Kenntnis der Säulenordnungen von großer Bedeutung für Giorgio Vasari. Der Sprung von den vagen theoretischen und historischen Ansätzen zur Architektur, die typisch für das 15. Jahrhundert sind, zur beeindruckenden Darstellung der Kunst- und Architekturgeschichte, die Vasari in der Einleitung zu seinen *Vite* bietet, ist augenfällig.[92] Sie zeugt von der beträchtlichen Wissensvermehrung jener Zeit, die durch die Medien Buch und Bild infolge der technischen Innovation des Buchdrucks erleichtert wurde. Vasaris Beschäftigung mit den Säulenordnungen ging mit seinem Versuch einher, die Kunstgeschichte in drei aufeinanderfolgende Stile (*maniere*) einzuteilen. Zur Demonstration der Exzellenz seiner eigenen Zeit, betonte er insbesondere Regelhaftigkeit, Ordnung und Proportion.[93] Diese Entwicklung des 16. Jahrhunderts war ein bedeutender Schritt hin zur Kultivierung eines Stils, der durch Standardisierung und exakte Regeln bestimmt wurde und den wir als Klassizismus bezeichnen können. Die besondere Tendenz zur Ordnung und Systematisierung war jedoch von den allmählichen Veränderungen in der Architektur und der Kultur im Allgemeinen in den vorangegangenen Jahrhunderten abhängig, einschließlich der mathematischen Innovationen, die sich seit der Gotik entwickelt hatten. Die Begegnung und Auseinandersetzung mit der antik-römischen Architektur in der Renaissance war stark von diesen jüngeren Veränderungen geprägt, die ihrerseits nicht als Wiedergeburt von etwas Antikem erklärt werden können.

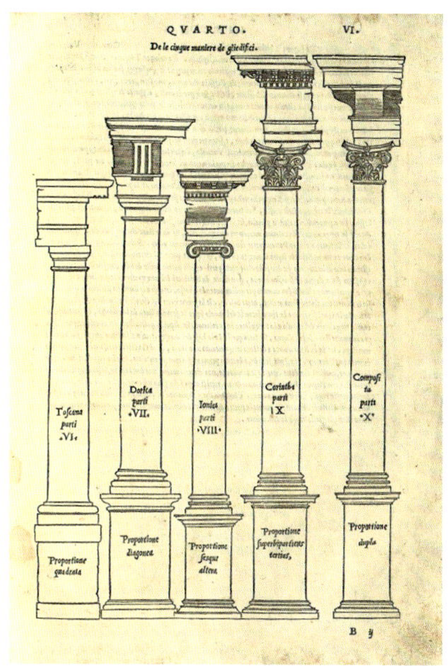

Abb. 25 Sebastiano Serlio, Die fünf Säulenordnungen. Holzschnitt in: ders., *Regole generali di architetura sopra le cinque maniere de gli edifici*, 4. Buch, Venedig, 1537, Fol. 6

Fig. 25 Sebastian Serlio, The five orders. Woodcut illustration in: Sebastiano Serlio, *Regole generali di architetura sopra le cinque maniere de gli edifici*, the fourth book of his architectural treatise, Venice, 1537, fol. 6

attempts to systematize the history of art in three successive styles, or *maniere*. In arguing for the excellence of his own time, he precisely emphasized rule, order, and proportion.[92] This development in the sixteenth century was a major step towards the cultivation of a style governed by standardization and exact rules, which we may term 'classicism'. But the profound urge to order was dependent on the gradual transformations within architecture, and culture in general, throughout the preceding centuries, including the mathematical innovations that, rather than having been brought about by the encounter with ancient Roman architecture, had developed from the Gothic period.

Die Historizität von Stilepochen

Die Bedeutung von Raffaels Brief ist nicht nur deshalb her-
ausragend, weil er zeigt, dass systematische und objektive
Studien der beispielhaften antiken römischen Architektur zu
dieser Zeit erst im Entstehen begriffen waren. Raffaels zöger-
liche und ungenaue Formulierungen und seine begrenzte
Terminologie in Bezug auf Stile sind ebenso aufschlussreich,
denn sie zeigen, dass selbst ein Künstler mit jahrelanger, aus-
geprägter Erfahrung mit dem architektonischen Erbe Roms
bei weitem nicht über jenen historischen Überblick verfügte,
wie er später durch Jahrhunderte historischer Gelehrsamkeit,
Bücher und Illustrationen erst geschaffen wurde. Raffaels
Brief macht deutlich, dass die Unterscheidung zwischen Gebäuden aus verschiedenen historischen Epochen um 1520
noch ein Novum war. Was Brunelleschi betrifft, so ist es
nicht nur unwahrscheinlich, dass er ein Jahrhundert vor Raffael die klassische Architektur Roms studierte. Wir können
auch feststellen, dass niemand zu seiner Zeit die Art von
Zeichnungen anfertige und Vermessungen durchführte, die
ihm später zugeschrieben wurden. Darüber hinaus wäre es
unpräzise anzunehmen, dass die Architekten und Humanisten des 15. Jahrhunderts an jene Gebäude dachten, die wir als
antik-römisch definieren, wenn sie über ihre Bewunderung
für etwas schrieben, das im *all'antica*-Stil gebaut wurde.

Wir müssen uns bewusst machen, dass die Menschen um
1500 weder über die Terminologie verfügten noch ein Auge
für Stil in der breiten Begriffskonzeption hatten, wie sie sich
ab dem 18. Jahrhundert entwickeln würde. Willibald Sauerländer zeigte bereits 1983 in einem Aufsehen erregenden Artikel, dass die Identifikation einer bestimmten Zeit – einer
bestimmten Kultur in einem bestimmten geografischen Ge-
biet – mit einem bestimmten Stil ein innovatives Konstrukt
war, das in der geschichtsbezogenen Denkweise zur Zeit

The Historicity of the Concept of a Period Style

Raphael's letter is of paramount importance not only because it shows that systematic and objective studies of exemplary ancient Roman architecture were only beginning to take place at the time. Raphael's hesitant, tentative, and inaccurate formulations and limited stylistic terminology are also revealing of the fact that even an artist with years of extensive experience in the architectural fabric of Rome did not cultivate historical knowledge comparable to what later centuries of scholarship and exposure to books and illustrations would bring about. Raphael's letter highlights that the very notion of distinguishing among buildings from various historical periods was a novelty around 1520. If we return to Brunelleschi, it is thus more than unlikely that he, a century prior to Raphael, had studied the classical architecture of Rome. Indeed, in Brunelleschi's day, nobody had yet made the kind of drawings and surveys Manetti would later attribute to the architect. But, of more general importance, it would be imprecise to believe that architects and humanists of the fifteenth century, when they wrote about their admiration for something made in an *all'antica* style, had in mind buildings we would define as ancient Roman.

We must bear in mind that around 1500 people had neither a terminology nor an eye for 'style', in the comprehensive sense of this concept as it has developed since the eighteenth century. In an eye-opening article published back in 1983, Willibald Sauerländer showed that the identification of a certain period of time – a certain culture in a certain geographical area – with a specific style had been an innovative construct rooted in the mindset of the time of Johann Joachim Winckelmann. In his *History of the Art of Antiquity* (1764), Winckelmann offered a pioneering categorization of four eras or stylistic phases of development in ancient Greek

Johann Joachim Winckelmanns verwurzelt ist. Die Kategorisierung von vier Epochen oder stilistischen Entwicklungsphasen der antiken griechischen Kunst in der *Geschichte der Kunst des Altertums* von 1764 war eine Pionierarbeit Winckelmanns. Eine solche Verbindung von Epochendenken und Stil war im 18. Jahrhundert neu und setzte sich erst im Verlauf des 19. Jahrhunderts durch.[94]

Die Unterscheidung von (Rede-)Stilen stammt ursprünglich aus der antiken Rhetorik; ab dem 16. Jahrhundert wurde der Begriff Stil oder auf Italienisch *maniera* für die bildende Künste übernommen.[95] Giorgio Vasaris kunsthistorische Darstellung geht von drei Stilen oder Manieren aus, die grob das 14., 15. und 16. Jahrhundert abdecken. Für Vasari war Stil jedoch synonym mit bewundernswerten künstlerischen Qualitäten konkreter Kunstwerke, und er erkannte *maniera* nur in Werken an, die er guthieß.[96] Winckelmanns Idee, einen bestimmten Stil, der in einer bestimmten Region vorherrschte, mit einer bestimmten historischen Epoche zu verknüpfen, war ein folgenreiches Novum für die kunsthistorische Disziplin. Die Kunsthistoriker und Kunsthistorikerinnen des 19. Jahrhunderts prägten Epochenbezeichnungen wie Renaissance oder Barock, an die wir uns später wie selbstverständlich gewöhnen sollten. Wenn Vasari im 16. Jahrhundert von *rinascità*, Wiedergeburt, sprach, machte der moderne Kunsthistoriker des 19. Jahrhunderts daraus ein *rinascimento*, eine Renaissance, und erweiterte damit das Stil- und Epochendenken zur kunsthistorischen Grundstruktur.

Wenn man bedenkt, dass die Verknüpfung einer bestimmten Zeit mit einem bestimmten Stil dem 18. und 19. Jahrhunderts zuzurechnen ist, wird deutlich, dass die Künstler des 15. Jahrhunderts die Antike nicht als eine klar definierte Zeitspanne mit einem bestimmten Stil auffassten oder sich dafür interessierten. Diese Erkenntnis kann uns helfen, eine unausgesprochene Gleichsetzung unseres Antikenkonzepts

art. Such a connection between a certain time span and a characteristic style was novel in Winckelmann's time and did not become current until the nineteenth century.[93]

The concept of style was originally related to ancient rhetoric, but by the sixteenth century the term 'style' or *maniera* was used with regard to visual art.[94] Giorgio Vasari's art-historical account is structured precisely by a notion of three styles or manners, roughly covering the fourteenth, fifteenth, and sixteenth centuries. But to Vasari, style was synonymous with an admirable artistic quality found in certain artworks, and he only recognized *maniera* in works of art that he approved of.[95] Winckelmann's notion of connecting one specific stylistic current within one specific geographic region to one specific period in history was, indeed, a novelty of major consequence for the art-historical discipline. It was nineteenth-century art historians who coined the period designations that we, by now, take for granted, for instance Renaissance or Baroque. Whereas in the sixteenth century Vasari had spoken of *rinascità*, or rebirth, nineteenth-century art historians spoke of a *rinascimento*, or *a* renaissance, ushering in the association of styles with periods – what would become a dominant structure in the history of art.

Given that this alignment of a specific period with a specific stylistic idiom belongs to the late eighteenth and nineteenth centuries, it becomes clear that fifteenth-century artists had neither an understanding of nor an interest in antiquity as a clearly defined time span characterized by one particular style. Acknowledging this will help us avoid tacitly equating their concept of antiquity with our own. By taking a critical stance towards the interpretation of the term 'classical' as signifying both a period and a style, as well as by facing the consequences of the fact that to a fifteenth-century person *antica* simply meant 'old', we may adjust our understanding of the Renaissance's relation to the past. And by

mit jenem des 15. Jahrhunderts zu vermeiden. Die kritische Auseinandersetzung mit der Übersetzung des Begriffs ›klassisch‹, der sowohl eine Zeitspanne als auch einen Stil bezeichnet, und die Anerkennung der Tatsache, dass *antica* für einen Menschen des 15. Jahrhunderts lediglich ›alt‹ bedeutete, ermöglichen uns, unser Verständnis des Verhältnisses zur Vergangenheit in der Renaissance anzupassen. Indem wir anerkennen, dass eine enge Verbindung zwischen Stil und Epoche erst in der Moderne, d. h. etwa ab dem 19. Jahrhundert, gebräuchlich wurde, können wir uns dem Konzept der Vergangenheit, das die Renaissance prägte, annähern und versuchen zu verstehen, was die Menschen tatsächlich meinten, wenn sie die Antike priesen. Gleichzeitig müssen wir eine Entwicklung nach 1500 anerkennen, die zu einer spezifischeren Kenntnis der Antike im modernen Sinne führte, was der Brief Raffaels eindrucksvoll bezeugt. Seine berühmte Stilanalyse der Reliefs des Konstantinbogens, in der er die Skulpturen als unbeholfen und kunstlos abtut, ist ein Beispiel dafür und lässt die Verbindung einer bestimmten Zeit mit einem bestimmten Stil bereits erahnen, die Sauerländer in der Moderne verankert.[97]

Meine Beobachtungen sind nicht als relativistische Gegenposition zu kunsthistorischen Projekten intendiert, die künstlerische Innovationen und Entwicklungen des 15. Jahrhunderts erforschen und ich stimme bedenkenlos Wölfflins berühmter Feststellung zu: »Nicht alles ist zu allen Zeiten möglich«.[98] Die Überlegungen dieses Essays sollen ein Beitrag zur Diskussion darüber leisten, welche Rolle der Antike bei der Herausbildung der Merkmale der Renaissance zukam. Aus dieser Perspektive ist es besonders wichtig zu berücksichtigen, was die Antike für die Menschen damals bedeutete und welcher Bezug und welche Sicht auf die Vergangenheit ihre Kunst und Architektur und ihren Enthusiasmus für den guten, antiken Stil, die *buona maniera antica*, bestimmten.

acknowledging that a close linkage between style and period only became manifest in modern times, meaning roughly in the nineteenth century, we may begin to approach the concept of the past that informed the Renaissance and to comprehend what fifteenth-century people meant when they eulogized 'antiquity'. At the same time, we must acknowledge a development after 1500 that brought about a more specific knowledge of antiquity in the modern sense, and, again, Raphael's letter is a major testimony to this. His famous stylistic analysis of the reliefs on the Arch of Constantine, wherein he dismissed the sculpture as awkward and artless, is a case in point, one that anticipated the connections of periods with styles, which Sauerländer would anchor in modern times.[96]

My observations here are not meant as a relativistic opposition to art-historical projects that have sought to characterize the artistic innovations and developments of the fifteenth century, and I readily agree with Wölfflin's famous observation that "not everything is possible at all times".[97] The reflections on the preceding pages are intended as a contribution to the discussion of the role played by antiquity in forming the key features of the Renaissance. What remains important is to keep track of what antiquity meant to people at the time, and what relation to and view of the past informed their art and architecture and their advocacy of the good, antique style, the *buona maniera antica*.

In fact, Panofsky never questioned whether the relationship to antiquity was really the Renaissance's sole defining trait. By synonymizing *antica* with 'classical', he implicitly reinforced the assumption that the period's inspiration from antiquity resulted in a classicist style. As he was looking for the similarities between the Renaissance and classical antiquity, he neglected the differences. However, if the Renaissance concept of antiquity ultimately differed from the one

Tatsächlich hinterfragte Panofsky nie, ob das Verhältnis zur Antike wirklich das einzige Kriterium zur Definition der Renaissance ist. Indem er *antica* mit *klassisch* gleichsetzte, bekräftigte er implizit die Annahme, dass die Inspiration durch die Antike zu einem klassizistischen Stil führte. Auf der Suche nach Gemeinsamkeiten zwischen der Renaissance und der Antike vernachlässigte er die vorhandenen Unterschiede. Wenn sich jedoch zeigt, dass der Antikenbegriff der Renaissance von dem abweicht, was Panofsky als selbstverständlich voraussetzte, verliert sein Modell an Überzeugungskraft.

In Abweichung von der bewährten kunsthistorischen Vorgangsweise immer neue Beispiele für die Bewunderung der antik-römischen Kultur im 15. Jahrhundert aufzuzeigen, ist meine Gegen- oder Parallelerzählung der Suche nach Beispielen für deren Ablehnung durch Künstler und Architekten der Renaissance gewidmet. Mit diesem Ansatz verschiebt sich der Fokus vom antiken Material, das in der Renaissance studiert wurde, zu dem, was keine Beachtung fand oder abgelehnt wurde. Es ist eine Erzählung darüber, was die Renaissance am antiken Rom nicht bewunderte, was die Künstler in ihren Zeichnungen übergingen, und somit eine Erzählung, die nicht die Ähnlichkeiten, sondern die Unterschiede zwischen der Renaissance und der Antike hervorhebt. Sie zielt darauf ab, die vielfältigen Abweichungen zwischen der Kunst und der Architektur der Epoche und der römischen Antike aufzuzeigen. Als Historiker gehen wir im Allgemeinen davon aus, dass sich die Vergangenheit niemals wiederholt, aber es ist sehr schwierig, exakt zu beschreiben, wie sich die visuelle Kultur der Renaissance von jener der römischen Antike unterscheidet. Eine Neubetrachtung des Begriffs *antico/antica* zeigt, dass dieser im 15. Jahrhundert nicht in unmittelbarer Abhängigkeit zur (klassischen) Antike stand. Die Hinterfragung eines Wertesystems, welches von den Kunsthistorikern und Kunsthistorikerinnen des 20. Jahrhunderts konstruiert

that Panofsky took for granted, then his model becomes less convincing.

Rather than adhering to the well-established art-historical strategy of exposing still further examples that speak to the fifteenth century's admiration of ancient Roman culture, my counter- or parallel narrative looks for cases in which Renaissance artists and architects rejected it. This approach does not focus on what ancient material they studied but rather on what ancient material they avoided studying. It is a narrative of what they did not admire from ancient Rome, what they chose not to draw, and thus a narrative that delineates not the similarities between the Renaissance and antiquity, but the dissimilarities. It aims to reveal the many ways in which the art and architecture of the period differed from those of Roman antiquity. As historians we tend to agree that the past is never repeated, but it is undeniably difficult to describe exactly how Renaissance visual culture diverged from that of ancient Rome. A reconsideration of the concept of *antico* or *antica* liberates the fifteenth-century notions of this concept from a dependence on (classical) antiquity. The rejection of a set of values constructed by art historians of the twentieth century, historically rooted in both Vasari and Burckhardt and forcefully propagated by Panofsky, may clear the way towards new questions in the field of art and architectural history. Moreover, the rejection of the hegemony of the ideal of classicism, which in many ways is remarkably close to the aesthetics of modernism, may prove productive for alternative characterizations of the cultural production of the Renaissance.

What if we substituted tracking the influence of classical antiquity on this period with highlighting the widespread strategies for producing naturalism; or if we focused on a theme such as cultural exchange or the material and technological conditions for the making of images and buildings?

wurde, das historisch sowohl bei Vasari als auch bei Burckhardt verwurzelt ist und von Panofsky mit Nachdruck propagiert wurde, kann den Weg für neuen Fragestellungen im Bereich der Kunst- und Architekturgeschichte eröffnen. Darüber hinaus könnte sich die Zurückweisung der Hegemonie des klassizistischen Ideals, das in vielerlei Hinsicht der Ästhetik der Moderne überraschend nahesteht, als produktiv für alternative Ansätze zur Erforschung der kulturellen Produktion der Renaissance erweisen.

Was wäre, wenn wir die auf der Rekonstruktion klassischantiker Einflüsse basierenden Charakterisierung der Epoche durch Betonung der weit verbreiteten Strategien zur Herstellung von Naturalismus ersetzen würden? Oder wenn wir uns auf Themen wie kulturellen Austausch oder die materiellen und technologischen Bedingungen für die Herstellung von Bildern und Gebäuden konzentrieren würden?

Wenn wir den Versuch hinterfragen, kunsthistorische Perioden durch ihre Bezugnahme auf die Antike oder durch den Grad des Klassizismus zu definieren, würde das auch die italienische Vormachtstellung in der kanonischen Hierarchie der Kunstgeschichte als weniger selbstverständlich erscheinen lassen. Nicht zuletzt von einem marginalen Standpunkt aus gesehen – was beispielsweise die Bedingung einer Kunsthistorikerin in Dänemark ist – könnte dieser Perspektivwechsel neue Ansätze für die Erforschung der in Nordeuropa produzierten Kunst ermöglichen. Ein gemeinsamer Nenner dieser Ansätze ist eine Pluralität von Perspektiven, die es ermöglicht, Beobachtungen in einer Weise zu teilen und auszutauschen, die noch vor wenigen Jahrzehnten undenkbar gewesen wäre. Eine kritische Auseinandersetzung mit der Suche nach Belegen für Wiederbelebungen der Antike in der Renaissance zielt also auf eine multiperspektivische Erweiterung unseres Verständnisses der Vergangenheit.

A questioning of the project of defining art-historical periods by their relation to antiquity or by the amount of classicism they display would, moreover, make the supremacy of the Italian Renaissance within the art-historical canon less self-evident. Not least from a marginal point of view – which, for instance, is the condition of an art historian in Denmark like me – this perspective could potentially bring about new approaches to the art produced in northern Europe and to our investigation of the past in general. A common denominator of these approaches is, perhaps, a multiplicity of viewpoints that allows observations to be interchanged in ways unthinkable only a couple of decades ago. A critical discussion of the quest to identify revivals of antiquity in the Renaissance is thus concerned with the opening up of new, inclusive understandings of the past.

* Danksagung: Ich danke Ulrich Pfisterer, Direktor des Zentralinstituts für Kunstgeschichte in München, sehr herzlich für die Einladung, als Panofsky-Professorin 2022 am Institut zu gastieren; ich habe nicht nur von der hervorragenden Bibliothek, sondern auch vom regen Austausch unter den wissenschaftlichen Mitarbeiter*innen des Instituts profitiert.

Die Forschungen, auf denen dieser Artikel basiert, habe ich im Rahmen meiner Tätigkeit an den Universitäten Aarhus und Kopenhagen in den letzten Jahrzehnten durchgeführt. Sie sind daher nicht zuletzt dem ständigen Austausch und der Diskussion mit meinen Kolleginnen und Kollegen sowie Studierenden zu verdanken. Der Artikel basiert teilweise auf früheren Arbeiten, insbesondere auf »Representing the Past: The Concept and Study of Antique Architecture in 15th-Century Italy«, in: *Analecta Romana Instituti Danici* 23 (1996): 83–116; *The Art of Transformation: Grotesques in Sixteenth-Century Italy* (Analecta Romana Instituti Danici, Supplementum, Bd. 49) (Rom, 2018) insbesondere: 149–217 und »Truth in Disguise: Allegorical Reinterpretations of Antiquity in Costumes and Masks of the Sixteenth Century«, in: Damiano Acciarino, Hrsg., *De re vestiaria: Antichità e moda nel Rinascimento* (Conegliano, 2022): 200–211.

1 Die Dominanz der italienischen Renaissance, einschließlich der Auswirkungen des ikonographischen Ansatzes nach Erwin Panofsky auf die nicht-narrative nordeuropäische Kunst, innerhalb der Kunstgeschichte wird von Svetlana Alpers aufschlussreich diskutiert. Vgl. Svetlana Alpers, *The Art of Describing. Dutch Art in the Seventeenth Century* (London, 1983): xvii–xxvii.

2 Erst mit F. A. Wolfs *Darstellung der Alterthums-Wissenschaft* (Berlin, 1807) wurde die Bezeichnung des antiken Griechenlands und Roms als ›klassisches Altertum‹ üblich; siehe Anthony Grafton, Glenn W. Most, Salvatore Settis, Hrsg., *The Classical Tradition* (Cambridge, MA, 2010): 205–206.

3 Heinrich Wölfflin, *Kunstgeschichtliche Grundbegriffe: Das Problem der Stilentwicklung in der neueren Kunst,* (München, 1915): 249–252; ders., *Die klassische Kunst: Eine Einführung in die italienische Renaissance* (München, 1899).

* Acknowledgements: My heartfelt thanks to Ulrich Pfisterer, Director of the Zentralinstitut für Kunstgeschichte in Munich, for the invitation to be a guest at the Institute as the 2022 Panofsky Professor; I have not only profited from the outstanding library but also from lively exchange among the Institute's many research fellows. The research on which this article is based took place as part of my work at Aarhus University and the University of Copenhagen over the last decades and is thus indebted to ongoing exchanges with my colleagues and students. The article is partially based on my previous work, especially "Representing the Past: The Concept and Study of Antique Architecture in 15th-Century Italy", in: *Analecta Romana Instituti Danici* 23 (1996): 83–116; *The Art of Transformation: Grotesques in Sixteenth-Century Italy* (Analecta Romana Instituti Danici, Supplementum, vol. 49) (Rome, 2018) especially: 149–217; and "Truth in Disguise: Allegorical Reintepretations of Antiquity in Costumes and Masks of the Sixteenth Century", in: Damiano Acciarino, ed., *De re vestiaria: Antichità e moda nel Rinascimento* (Conegliano, 2022): 200–211.

1 The dominance of the Italian Renaissance, including the consequences of the Panofskian iconographical approach on northern European, non-narrative art, is discussed with insight in Svetlana Alpers, *The Art of Describing: Dutch Art in the Seventeenth Century* (London, 1983): xvii–xxvii.

2 It was with F. A. Wolf, *Darstellung der Alterthums-Wissenschaft* (Berlin, 1807), that the designation of ancient Greece and Rome as "classical antiquity" became common; see Anthony Grafton, Glenn W. Most, Salvatore Settis eds., *The Classical Tradition* (Cambridge, MA, 2010): 205–206.

3 Heinrich Wölfflin, *Principles of Art History: The Problem of the Development of Style in Early Modern Art* [1915], Jonathan Blower, trans., essays by Evonne Levy and Tristan Weddigen (The Getty Research Institute: Texts and Documents) (Los Angeles, 2015): 310–312; idem, *Classic Art: An Introduction to the Italian Renaissance* [1899], Peter and Linda Murray, trans. (London, 1952).

4 Erwin Panofsky, *Renaissance and Renaissances in Western Art* (New York, NY, 1972) [1960]. The book was based on a

4 Erwin Panofsky, *Renaissance and Renascences in Western Art* (New York, NY, 1972) [1960]. Das Buch basiert auf einer Reihe von Vorlesungen, die Panofsky 1952 auf Einladung der Universität Uppsala in Stockholm hielt und die zuerst 1960 in der Reihe Figura von Almqvist und Wiksells, Gebers Forlag AB in Stockholm erschienen sind.

5 Panofsky, *Renaissance and Renascences* (wie Anm. 4): 10–21.

6 Jacob Burckhardt, *Die Cultur der Renaissance in Italien: Ein Versuch* [1860], Mikkel Mangold, Hrsg., auf der Grundlage der Vorarbeiten von Kenji Hara und Hiroyuki Numata (Jacob Burckhardt, *Werke: Kritische Gesamtausgabe*, Bd. 4) (München, 2018): 92.

7 Erwin Panofsky, »Die Perspektive als ›symbolische Form‹«, in: *Vorträge der Bibliothek Warburg 1924–1925* (Berlin, 1927): 258–331.

8 Ders., *Early Netherlandish Painting*, 2 Bd. (Cambridge, MA, 1953) Bd. 1: 3–20.

9 Ders., *Renaissance and Renascences*: 113.

10 Aby Warburg, *Die Erneuerung der heidnischen Antike: Kulturwissenschaftliche Beiträge zur Geschichte der europäischen Renaissance*. Reprint der von Gertrud Bing unter Mitarbeit von Fritz Rougemont edierten Ausgabe von 1932. Neu herausgegeben von Horst Bredekamp und Michael Diers (Gesammelte Schriften. Studienausgabe, H. Bredekamp et al., Hrsg.) (Berlin, 1988). In »Artistic Survival: Panofsky vs. Warburg and the Exorcism of Impure Time«, in: *Common Knowledge* 9 (2003): 273–285, kritisiert Georges Didi-Huberman die Suche nach Ursprüngen und Wiederbelebungen in ikonographischen Studien Panofskys und seiner Nachfolgerinnen und Nachfolger. Demnach konnten Gombrich, Panofsky und Saxl die zentrale Einsicht von Warburgs Konzept des Nachlebens entweder nicht erkennen oder schoben sie bewusst beiseite. Didi-Huberman beschäftigt sich jedoch nicht mit den schriftlichen und visuellen Zeugnissen des historischen Bewusstseins oder der Konzeption des *antico*-Begriffs im Italien des 15. Jahrhundert.

11 Didi-Huberman, »Artistic Survival« (wie Anm. 10): 273–285; Alexander Nagel und Christopher S. Wood, »Toward a New Model of Renaissance Anachronism«, in: *The Art*

series of lectures held in Stockholm in 1952, organized by the University of Uppsala, and was first published in the series *Figura* by Almqvist & Wiksells, Gebers Forlag AB in Stockholm, 1960.

5   Panofsky, *Renaissance and Renascences* (see fn. 4): 10–21.

6   Jacob Burckhardt, *The Civilization of the Renaissance in Italy* [1860], S.G.C. Middlemore, trans. (The Floating Press, 2014) [1878]: 112.

7   Erwin Panofsky, *Perspective as Symbolic Form* [1927], Christopher S. Wood, trans. (New York, NY, 1991).

8   Erwin Panofsky, *Early Netherlandish Painting*, 2 vols. (Cambridge, MA, 1953), vol. 1: 3–20.

9   Panofsky, *Renaissance and Renascences* (see fn. 4): 113.

10   Aby Warburg, *Die Erneuerung der heidnischen Antike: Kulturwissenshaftliche Beiträge zur Geschichte der europäischen Renaissance*. Reprint of the 1932 edition edited by Getrud Bing with the collaboration of Fritz Rougemont. Newly edited by Horst Bredekamp and Michael Diers, (Gesammelte Schriften. Studienausgabe, H. Bredekamp et al., ed.) (Berlin, 1988). In "Artistic Survival: Panofsky vs. Warburg and the Exorcism of Impure Time", in *Common Knowledge* 9 (2003): 273–285, Georges Didi-Huberman presents a critique of the search for origins and revivals in Panofskian and post-Panofskian iconographic studies. Didi-Huberman suggests that Gombrich, Panofsky, and Saxl either were blind to or deliberately excised the insight embedded in Warburg's concept of *Nachleben*. Didi-Huberman is not, however, concerned with the historical consciousness formulated or visualized by fifteenth-century Italians nor with their understanding of the concept of *antico*.

11   Didi-Huberman, "Artistic Survival" (see fn. 10): 273–285; Alexander Nagel and Christopher S. Wood, "Toward a New Model of Renaissance Anachronism", in: *Art Bulletin* 87 (2005): 403–415; A. Nagel and Christopher S. Wood, *Anachronic Renaissance* (New York, 2010); Keith F. Moxey, "What Time is it in the History of Art?", in: Dan Karlholm and Keith F. Moxey, eds., *Time in the History of Art: Temporality, Chronology, and Anachrony* (London, 2020): 26–41; for a classic, if I may, discussion of the problems implicit in the

Bulletin 87 (2005): 403–415; Alexander Nagel und Christopher S. Wood, *Anachronic Renaissance* (New York, 2010); Keith P. F. Moxey, »What Time is it in the History of Art?«, in: Dan Karlholm, Keith P. F. Moxey, Hrsg., *Time in the History of Art: Temporality, Chronology, and Anachrony* (London, 2020): 26–41. Zur grundlegenden Diskussion der Probleme, die mit der Suche nach kulturellen Ursprüngen verbunden sind, siehe Michel Foucault [1971] »Nietzsche, Genealogy, History«, in: Donald F. Bouchard, Hrsg., *Language, Counter-Memory, Practice: Selected Essays and Interviews* (Ithaca, NY, 2021): 139–164.

12 Da die bildenden Künste und Architektur im Betrachtungszeitraum fast ausschließlich von Männern betrieben wurden, verzichte ich im Folgenden in diesem Zusammenhang auf die weibliche Form.

13 Panofsky, *Renaissance and Renascences* (wie Anm. 4): 18–35; der Begriff ist erstmals im späten 14. Jahrhundert nachweisbar. Siehe Ulrich Pfisterer, *Donatello und die Entdeckung der Stile 1430–1445* (Römische Studien der Bibliotheca Hertziana, Bd. 17) (München, 2002): 85.

14 Beispielhaft für Panofskys Übersetzung von *antico* und *all'antica* als *klassisch* siehe ders., *Renaissance and Renascences* (wie Anm. 4): 19f.

15 Ich möchte an dieser Stelle dem leider bereits verstorbenen Salvatore Camporeale für unsere Diskussionen über das Konzept *all'antica* danken.

16 Die mittelalterlichen Quellen der Humanisten und insbesondere Brunelleschis, der in der *all'antica* Manier baute, analysiert Ernst H. Gombrich in seinem wichtigen Artikel »From the Revival of Letters to the Reform of the Arts: Niccolò Niccoli and Filippo Brunelleschi« [1967], in: ders., *Gombrich on the Renaissance*, Vol. 3: *The Heritage of Apelles* (London, 1976): 93–110. Es war allerdings nicht Gombrichs Ziel, die Übersetzung von *antica* in Frage zu stellen oder die den Künstlern und Humanisten des 15. Jahrhunderts zugeschriebene generelle Intention, die römische Antike zu imitieren und eine klassische Kunstsprache zu pflegen, zu hinterfragen. Trotz seines Titels ist Gombrichs Artikel »The Style all'antica: Imitation and Assimilation«, in: *Renaissance and Mannerism* (International Congress of the

search for cultural origins, see the essay by Michel Foucault [1971] translated to "Nietzsche, Genealogy, History", in: *Language, Counter-Memory, Practice: Selected Essays and Interviews*, Donald F. Bouchard, ed. (Ithaca, NY, 2021): 139–164.

12 Panofsky, *Renaissance and Renascences* (see fn. 4): 18–35; the earliest appearance of the term is in the late fourteenth century. See Ulrich Pfisterer, *Donatello und die Entdeckung der Stile 1430–1445* (Römische Studien der Bibliotheca Hertziana, vol. 17) (Munich, 2002): 85.

13 For examples of Panofsky's translation of *antico* and *all'antica* to 'classical' (see fn. 4): 19–20.

14 I am grateful to the late Salvatore Camporeale for discussing the concept of *all'antica* with me.

15 The medieval sources of the humanists and of Brunelleschi, working in an *all'antica* manner, are foregrounded by Ernst H. Gombrich in his important article, "From the Revival of Letters to the Reform of the Arts: Niccolò Niccoli and Filippo Brunelleschi" [1967], in: *Gombrich on the Renaissance*, vol. 3: *The Heritage of Apelles* (London, 1976): 93–110. It was, however, not Gombrich's aim to question the translation of *antica*, nor to discuss the general intention on the part of fifteenth-century artists and humanists to imitate Roman antiquity and to cultivate a classical language of art; despite its title, Gombrich's article, "The Style *all'antica*: Imitation and Assimilation", in: *Renaissance and Mannerism* (International Congress of the History of Art) (Princeton, NJ): 31–41, is less relevant in our context, as it analyses the concept of imitation from the perspective of rhetorical theory. Here, Gombrich was concerned with the principles that Renaissance artists such as Giulio Romano had extracted from ancient Roman art, as well as with distinguishing between assimilation and imitation. But he did not engage in a discussion of how they defined antiquity or *all'antica* in their time.

16 Panofsky, *Renaissance and Renascences* (see fn. 4): 34–35.

17 Giorgio Vasari, "Proemio delle vite", in: Rosanna Bettarini and Paola Barocchi eds., *Le vite de' più eccellenti pittori, scultori e architettori nelle redazioni del 1550 e 1568* (Florence, 1967) vol. 2, Testo: 29. "Ma perché più agevolmente

History of Art) (Princeton, NJ): 31–41, in unserem Zusammenhang weniger relevant, da er den Begriff der Nachahmung von einem rhetorischen Ausgangspunkt aus betrachtet. Gombrich befasste sich mit den Prinzipien, die Renaissancekünstler wie Giulio Romano von der römischen Kunst abzuleiten versuchten, und mit der Unterscheidung von Assimilation und Imitation. Eine Diskussion über die zeitgenössische Definition der Antike oder von *all'antica* führt er nicht.

17 Panofsky, *Renaissance and Renascences* (wie Anm. 4): 34–35.

18 »Ma perché più agevolmente s'intenda quello che io chiami vecchio et antico, antiche furono le cose, innanzi a Costantino, di Corinto, d'Atene e di Roma e d'altre famosissime città, fatte fino a sotto Nerone, ai Vespasiani, Traiano, Adriano et Antonino, perciò che l'altre si chiamano vec[c] hie che da Salvestro in qua furono poste in opera da un certo residuo de Greci, i quali più tosto tignere che dipignere sapevano«, Giorgio Vasari, »Proemio delle vite«, in: Rosanna Bettarini und Paola Barocchi, Hrsg., *Le vite de' più eccellenti pittori, scultori e architettori nelle redazioni del 1550 e 1568* (Florenz, 1967) Vol. 2, Testo: 29.

19 Ein Zeitgenosse Vasaris, der sich ebenfalls mit den Begriffen *antik* und *alt* (*antigo* und *velho*) auseinandersetzte, war der Portugiese Francisco de Hollanda, der sich 1538–1547 in Rom aufhielt und nach seiner Rückkehr seine theoretischen Beobachtungen publizierte; siehe Francisco de Hollanda, *Da pintura antiga*, Angel Gonzáles Garcia intr. und not. (Porto, 1964) I. xi: 79. Auch de Hollandas sorgfältige Begriffsklärung zeigt, dass die Unterscheidung noch nicht allgemein üblich war. Wie David Summers in »Michelangelo on Architecture«, in: *Art Bulletin* 54 (1972): 146–157, zeigt, spiegeln Francisco de Hollandas Beobachtungen die Ideen Michelangelos und seines theoretischen Umfelds wider; Peter Burkes Beobachtung in seinem einflussreichen Werk *The Renaissance Sense of the Past* (London, 1969) über das, was er eine im Mittelalter herrschende »historische Unschuld« nennt, scheint auch im frühen 16. Jahrhundert noch zutreffend zu sein, so dass die Zäsur zwischen Mittelalter und Renaissance weniger dramatisch ausfällt, als von der Forschung oft suggeriert: 2.

s'intenda quello che io chiami vecchio et antico, antiche furono le cose, innanzi a Costantino, di Corinto, d'Atene e di Roma e d'altre famosissime città, fatte fino a sotto Nerone, ai Vespasiani, Traiano, Adriano et Antonino, perciò che l'altre si chiamano vec[c]hie che da S. Salvestro in qua furono poste in opera da un certo residuo de Greci, i quali più tosto tignere che dipignere sapevono".

18 Contemporary with Vasari, another insightful writer who discussed the terms 'antique' and 'old' (*antigo* and *velho*) was the Portuguese Francisco de Hollanda, who, upon his return home from a stay in Rome that spanned from 1538 to 1547, compiled his theoretical observations, see Francisco de Holanda, *Da pintura antiga*, Angel Gonzáles Garcia intr. & not. (Porto, 1964) I. xi: 79. Again, Francisco de Hollanda's careful clarification of terms indicates that this was not yet common knowledge at the time. As David Summers has shown in "Michelangelo on Architecture", *Art Bulletin* 54 (1972): 146–157. Francisco de Hollanda's observations may very well reflect the ideas of Michelangelo and his theoretical environment; Peter Burke's observation in his influential *The Renaissance Sense of the Past* (London, 1969) of what he calls a "historical innocence" current to the Middle Ages, seems to have still been fitting in the early sixteenth century, making the watershed between the medieval period and the Renaissance less dramatic than scholars have often wanted it to be: 2.

19 Cesare Vecellio, *De gli Habiti Antichi e Modérni di Diversi Parti di Mondo* (Venice, 1590).

20 A selection of influential authors sceptical towards Brunelleschi's trip to Rome and the supposed impact of the ancient ruins on his buildings includes Howard Saalman in his introduction to Brunelleschi's biography: Antonio di Tuccio Manetti, *The Life of Brunelleschi*, H. Saalman ed., Catherine Enggass, trans.(University Park, PA, 1970): 26–30; Gombrich, "From the Revival of Letters" (see fn. 15): 103; Howard Burns, "Quattrocento Architecture and the Antique: Some Problems", in: *Classical Influences on European Culture A. D. 500–1500*, R. R. Bolgar, ed. (Cambridge, 1971): 277–284; John Onians, *Bearers of Meaning: The Classical Orders in Antiquity, the Middle Ages, and the*

20 Cesare Vecellio, *De gli Habiti Antichi e Modérni di Diversi Parti di Mondo* (Venedig, 1590).

21 Zu den wichtigsten kunsthistorischen Stimmen, die Brunelleschis legendäre Reise nach Rom und den Einfluss der antiken Ruinen auf seine Bauten mit Skepsis betrachten, zählen Howard Saalman in seiner Einleitung zur Brunelleschi Biografie: Antonio di Tuccio Manetti, *The Life of Brunelleschi*, H. Saalman, Hg., Catherine Enggass, Übers, (University Park, PA, 1970): 26–30; Gombrich, »From the Revival of Letters«, 103 (wie Anm. 16); Howard Burns, »Quattrocento Architecture and the Antique: Some Problems«, in: R. R. Bolgar, Hg., *Classical Influences on European Culture A. D. 500–1500*, (Cambridge, 1971): 277–284; John Onians, *Bearers of Meaning: The Classical Orders in Antiquity, the Middle Ages, and the Renaissance* (Princeton, NJ, 1988): 130–136; Hans Tietze, »Romanische Kunst und Renaissance«, in: *Vorträge der Bibliothek Warburg 1926–1927* (Leipzig, 1930): 52.

22 Eine folgenreiche Kritik an der konventionellen kunsthistorischen Darstellung der Renaissance als Wiederbelebung der Antike bieten Nagel und Wood, *Anachronic Renaissance* (wie Anm. 11). In zahlreichen Fallstudien zeigen die Autoren das komplexe Verhältnis der Renaissance zu Vorbildern aus verschiedenen Epochen der Vergangenheit, in erheblichem Maße auch der Nachantike, auf. Für weitere Beispiele von Studien der letzten Jahrzehnte, die die mittelalterlichen Quellen Brunelleschis diskutieren, siehe Uta Schedler, *Filippo Brunelleschi: Synthese von Antike und Mittelalter* (Petersberg, 2004); und David Hemsoll, *Emulating Antiquity: Renaissance Buildings from Brunelleschi to Michelangelo* (New Haven, CT, 2019).

23 Antonio Manetti, *Vita di Filippo Brunelleschi*, Carlachiara Perrone, Hg. (Rom, 1992): 68: »Intorno alle quali opera Filippo stette molti anni [...]«, und: 79. Brunelleschi kehrte 1419 nach Florenz zurück.

24 Der große Kenner der Renaissance-Architekturzeichnung nach der Antike, Hubertus Günther, dem wir den kanonischen Überblick *Das Studium der antiken Architektur in den Zeichnungen der Hochrenaissance* (Tübingen, 1988) verdanken, mahnt bei der wörtlichen Auslegung von Manettis

Renaissance (Princeton, NJ, 1988): 130–136; Hans Tietze, "Romanische Kunst und Renaissance", in: *Vorträge der Bibliothek Warburg 1926–1927* (Leipzig, 1930): 52.

21 An eye-opening critique of the conventional art-historical narrative of the Renaissance as a revival of antiquity is offered by Nagel and Wood, *Anachronic Renaissance* (see fn. 11), who analyse an extensive series of cases highlighting the complex relation of the Renaissance to models from various periods of the past, to a considerable extent also post-antique ones; for other examples of discussions over the last decades concerning the medieval sources of Brunelleschi, see Uta Schedler, *Filippo Brunelleschi: Synthese von Antike und Mittelalter* (Petersberg, 2004); and David Hemsoll, *Emulating Antiquity: Renaissance Buildings from Brunelleschi to Michelangelo* (New Haven, CT, 2019).

22 Antonio Manetti, *Vita di Filippo Brunelleschi*, Carlachiara Perrone, ed. (Rome, 1992): 68: "Intorno alle quali opera Filippo stette molti anni [...]", and: 79. Brunelleschi returned to Florence in 1419.

23 The great scholar of Renaissance architectural drawings of ancient architecture, Hubertus Günther, who authored the masterly survey *Das Studium der antiken Architektur in den Zeichnungen der Hochrenaissance* (Tübingen, 1988), was cautious about taking Manetti's account too literally. Nevertheless, he was generally uncritical towards assertions that Brunelleschi had undertaken thorough investigations and even excavations of ancient ruins, and he did not focus on how such investigations differed from modern understandings and practices: 19–21, thus accepting that Brunelleschi had acquired a familiarity with the ancient Roman buildings through his studies in the city. See also Günther's condensed account of major portions of his research in *Die Renaissance der Antike* (Weimar, 1997): 19. In the recent contribution to the research on Brunelleschi's architecture, Hemsoll, *Emulating Antiquity* (see fn. 21): 32; also accepts the sources' assertions, as he states that Brunelleschi "allegedly" studied the ancient Roman buildings.

24 Manetti, *Vita* (see fn. 22): 68–69: "col suo vedere sottile conobbe bene la distinzione di ciascuno spezie, come

Darstellungen zur Vorsicht. Dennoch steht er den Behauptungen bezüglich Brunelleschis gründlichen Untersuchungen und sogar Ausgrabungen antiker Ruinen in Rom im Allgemeinen unkritisch gegenüber und er stellt auch nicht die Frage, inwiefern sich solche Untersuchungen vom modernen Verständnis und der modernen Praxis unterscheiden: 19–21. Somit akzeptiert Günther die allgemeine Annahme, dass Brunelleschi sich einen Überblick über die antiken Gebäude in Rom verschaffte. Siehe auch Günthers konzise Darstellung zentraler Teile seiner Forschungen in *Die Renaissance der Antike* (Weimar, 1997): 19. In einem neueren Beitrag zur Erforschung von Brunelleschis Architektur übernimmt auch Hemsoll, *Emulating Antiquity* (wie Anm. 22): 32, die Behauptungen der Quellen, wenn er feststellt, dass Brunelleschi »angeblich« die antiken römischen Bauten studiert habe.

25 Manetti, *Vita* (wie Anm. 23): 68–69: »col suo vedere sottile conobbe bene la distinzione di ciascuno spezie, come furono Ionice, Dorice, Toscane, Corinte e Attice, e usò a' tempi ed a' luoghi della maggiore parte, dove gli pareva meglio [...]«. In »Filippo Brunelleschi: Capital Studies«, *Art Bulletin* 40 (1958): 115, stellte Howard Saalman fest, dass Brunelleschi eine vereinfachte Version des korinthischen Kapitells bevorzugte, die jenen Kapitellen ähnelt, die Giotto in der Peruzzi-Kapelle von Santa Croce gemalt hatte, anstatt korinthische Kapitelle aus dem antiken Rom zu imitieren. Burns kommentiert diese Beobachtung: »Despite the fact that he must often have seen the antique type, he preferred to use a simplified and rationalized version of it«, in »Quattrocento Architecture« (wie Anm. 21): 279. Auch diesem Kommentar liegt also die Annahme zugrunde, dass Brunelleschi das, was wir als antik-römische Architektur verstehen, wiederbeleben wollte und dabei ein ausgeprägtes historisches Bewusstsein hatte.

26 In seiner Einleitung zu den *Vite* verweist Vasari auf die mittelalterlichen florentinischen Kirchen, die von Brunelleschi für modellhaft erachtet wurden: »Pippo di ser Brunellesco non si sdegnò di servirsene per modello nel fare la Chiesa di Spirito e quella di Lorenzo«, Vasari, *Vite* (wie

furono Ionice, Dorice, Toscane, Corinte e Attice, e usò a'
tempi ed a' luoghi della maggiore parte, dove gli pareva
meglio [...]"; Howard Saalman, "Filippo Brunelleschi: Capital Studies", *Art Bulletin* 40 (1958): 115, observed that
Brunelleschi had preferred a simplified version of the
Corinthian capital, similar to the ones painted by Giotto in
Santa Croce's Peruzzi Chapel, rather than imitating Corinthian capitals from ancient Rome; Burns, "Quattrocento
Architecture" (see fn. 20): 279, commented on Saalman's
observation: "Despite the fact that he must often have seen
the antique type, he preferred to use a simplified and
rationalised version of it". Burns thus took it for granted
that Brunelleschi had wanted to revive what we understand as ancient Roman architecture, and he did not question that the architect had operated with a well-defined
historical consciousness.

25 In his introduction to the *Vite*, Vasari points to the medieval Florentine churches as sources that Brunelleschi
deemed to be worthy models (see fn. 17): 24: "Pippo di ser
Brunellesco non si sdegnò di servirsene per modello nel
fare la Chiesa di S. Spirito e quella di S. Lorenzo [...]";
Vasari's observation of Brunelleschi's Florentine sources
of inspiration has been discussed already by Tietze, "Romanische Kunst und Renaissance" (see fn. 20): 52–53.

26 Note that the dome of the baptistery is a double-vault
construction, as mentioned by Manetti, *Vita* (see fn. 22): 85,
and by Vasari in his "Life of Andrea Tafi" in the *Vite* (see
fn. 17): 74. A model for Brunelleschi's double-vaulted dome
for the cathedral was thus similarly close at hand.

27 Gombrich, "From the Revival of Letters" (see fn. 15): 106; in
Renaissance and Renascences (see fn. 4): 40. Panofsky was
fully aware of this line of research, but it was not crucial to
his argument; Onians, *Bearers of Meaning* (see fn. 20): 130,
emphatically writes that "Given the evidence, the notion
that Brunelleschi wished to revived Roman architecture
seems at best improbable and at worst absurd".

28 In his propagation of this observation, Burns, "Quattrocento Architecture" n. 5 (see fn. 20): 277, refers to Saalman's
frequent assertions that Brunelleschi's works "contain no
specific motifs derived directly from the antique"; see also

Anm. 18): 24. Vasaris Beobachtung der florentinischen Inspirationsquellen Brunelleschis wurde bereits von Tietze diskutiert, »Romanische Kunst und Renaissance« (wie Anm. 21): 52–53.

27 Es ist bemerkenswert, dass es sich bei der Kuppel des Baptisteriums um eine Doppelschalenkonstruktion handelt, wie von Manetti *Vita* (wie Anm. 23): 85, und von Vasari in seinem »Leben des Andrea Taf« in den *Vite* (wie Anm. 18): 74, erwähnt wird. Ein architektonisches Modell für Brunelleschis Kuppel war also ebenfalls in greifbarer Nähe.

28 Gombrich, »From the Revival of Letters« (wie Anm. 16): 106. In *Renaissance and Renascences* (wie Anm. 4): 40, erwähnt Panofsky diese Forschungsrichtung, berücksichtigt sie jedoch nicht in seiner Argumentation. Onians betont: »Given the evidence, the notion that Brunelleschi wished to revive Roman architecture seems at best improbable and at worst absurd«, *Bearers of Meaning* (wie Anm. 21): 130.

29 Burns bezieht sich in »Quattrocento Architecture« auf Saalman, dem er die Aussage zuschreibt, dass in Brunelleschis Werk keine Motive vorkämen, die direkt der Antike entstammen, »Quattrocento Architecture« N. 5 (wie Anm. 21): 277. Dazu siehe auch Saalmans Einleitung in *Life of Brunelleschi* (wie Anm. 21): 30. Zum erneuerten Interesse an Brunelleschis mittelalterlichen Quellen (wie Anm. 22).

30 Hans Belting, »The Double Perspective: Arab Mathematics and Renaissance Art«, in: *Third Text* 24 (2010): 521–527; Jacob Wamberg, »Ghiberti, Alberti, and the Modernity of Gothic«, *Analecta Romana Instituti Danici* 21 (1993): 173 ff.; Ders., *Landscape as World Picture: Tracing Cultural Evolution in Images* (2005), Gaye Kynoch, Übers., 2 Bd. (Aarhus, 2009), Bd. 2: 51–116. Wenn der Verdacht, dass Manetti die Neuerungen seiner eigenen Zeit seinem Helden zuschreibt, ernstgenommen wird, kann sogar Brunelleschis Entwicklung der mathematisch konstruierten Perspektive in Frage gestellt werden. Uns liegen keine Zeichnungen vor, die seine entscheidende Rolle dabei bestätigen könnten. Sein Konkurrenzrelief für den Wettbewerb um die Gestaltung der Türen des Baptisteriums bezeugt keinerlei Anzeichen von Interesse an einer solchen räumlichen

Saalman's introduction in *Life of Brunelleschi* (see fn. 20): 30; for renewed attention to Brunelleschi's medieval sources (see fn. 21).

29 Hans Belting, "The Double Perspective Arab Mathematics and Renaissance Art", in: *Third Text* 24 (2010): 521–527; Jacob Wamberg, "Ghiberti, Alberti, and the Modernity of Gothic", *Analecta Romana Instituti Danici* 21 (1993): 173 ff.; idem, *Landscape as World Picture: Tracing Cultural Evolution in Images* (2005) Gaye Kynoch, trans., 2 vols. (Aarhus, 2009) vol. 2: 51–116. If we may take further our notion that Manetti was re-attributing to his hero the novelties of his own age, even Brunelleschi's development of mathematically constructed perspective may be questioned. Again, we have no drawings confirming his crucial role in this. His relief for the competition for the baptistery doors shows no signs of interest in such spatial illusion; and it is noteworthy that Alberti does not mention him when he presents the perspectival construction in *De pictura*, in the mid-1430s. If Brunelleschi had actually been admired at the time as the 'inventor' of this, would not Alberti, who praises Brunelleschi's achievements regarding the cathedral dome, have been likely to mention him in connection with perspective, as well? I am grateful to Hans Bendixen, an art history student at the University of Copenhagen who drew my attention to this parallel questioning of Manetti's reliability, coinciding with the doubts towards Brunelleschi's studies of ancient Roman architecture.

30 This is convincingly put forward by Onians, *Bearers of Meaning* (see fn. 20): 133.

31 Gombrich, "From the Revival of Letters" (see fn. 15): 104, n. 55, presents the sources, the earliest of which dates back to the fourteenth century, with the chronicler Giovanni Villani and the chancellor Coluccio Salutati identifying the baptistery as an ancient temple of Mars; Nagel and Wood, *Anachronic Renaissance* (see fn. 11), include an illustration (13.1.) by the Florentine artisan Marco di Bartolommeo Rustici, who claimed that the baptistery had been built in the time of Augustus; the labelling of the baptistery as an ancient temple was reiterated by Vasari in the middle of the sixteenth century, see *Vite* (see fn. 17): 25.

Illusion und es ist bemerkenswert, dass Alberti ihn in
seiner Vorstellung der Perspektivkonstruktion in *De pictura* Mitte der 1430er Jahre nicht erwähnt. Sollte Brunelleschi damals tatsächlich als ›Erfinder‹ bewundert worden
seien, wäre es dann nicht auch für Alberti, der Brunelleschis Leistungen bei der Domkuppel hervorhebt, naheliegend gewesen, ihn in Zusammenhang mit der Perspektive
zu erwähnen? Ich bin Hans Bendixen, Student der Kunstgeschichte an der Universität Kopenhagen, dankbar, dass
er mich auf diese Parallellinie der Diskussion der Zuverläs-
sigkeit Manettis aufmerksam gemacht hat, die mit den
Zweifeln bezüglich Brunelleschis Studien der antiken
römischen Architektur in engem Zusammenhang steht.

31 Vgl. Onians, *Bearers of Meaning* (wie Anm. 21): 133.

32 Die frühesten, von Gombrich vorgelegten Quellen, stam-
    men aus dem 14. Jahrhundert. Ihnen zufolge identifizier-
    ten der Chronist Giovanni Villani und der Kanzler Coluc-
    cio Salutati das Baptisterium als antiken Marstempel.
    Siehe Gombrich, »From the Revival of Letters« (wie
    Anm. 16): 104, Anm. 55. Nagel und Wood besprechen eine
    Illustration (13.1.) des Florentiner Kunsthandwerkers
    Marco di Bartolommeo Rustici, der behauptete, dass das
    Baptisterium zur Zeit des Augustus erbaut worden sei,
    Nagel und Wood, *Anachronic Renaissance* (wie Anm. 11).
    Die Bezeichnung des Baptisteriums als antiker Tempel
    wurde von Vasari noch in der Mitte des 16. Jahrhunderts
    wiederholt; vgl. Vasari, *Vite* (wie Anm. 18): 25.

33 Es wird nach wie vor häufig davon ausgegangen, dass
    Künstler des 15. Jahrhunderts das Mittelalter bewusst als
    Modell wählten, d. h., sie wussten, dass ihre Modelle einer
    nachantiken Periode entstammten. Siehe z. B. die aktuelle
    Studie von Brian A. Curran, »The Renaissance: The ›Disco-
    very‹ of Ancient Rome«, in: C. Holleran und A. Claridge,
    Hrsg., *A Companion to the City of Rome* (Hoboken, NJ,
    2018): 643–671. Curran konzentriert sich auf die Frage, wie
    das Interesse an der Antike zustande kam und wie es sich
    äußerte. Dabei stellt er fest, dass die Florentiner das Bap-
    tisterium »zurückdatierten«. Die grundlegendere Frage
    danach, was mit *all'antica* gemeint war, wird in diesem
    Text jedoch nicht erörtert. Insofern impliziert dieser

32 It is still regularly taken for granted that fifteenth-century
artists and architects chose the Middle Ages as their model
quite consciously, that is, that they knew that their models
dated to a post-antique period, see for instance, the recent
survey, Brian A. Curran, "The Renaissance: The 'Discovery'
of Ancient Rome", in: C. Holleran & A. Claridge, eds., *A
Companion to the City of Rome* (Hoboken, NJ, 2018): 643–
671. Curran focuses on how the interest in antiquity took
place and on mapping how it manifested itself, and he
observes that the Florentines 'backdated' the baptistery.
But it is not within the scope of the author's interest to
discuss in more general terms what they meant by *all'antica*. This approach implies a projection of a scientific and
historically conscious approach back on the Renaissance's
use of the past rather than a questioning of what their
concept of antiquity involved; Günther, *Die Renaissance
der Antike* (see fn. 23): 7, suggests that Romanesque architecture was deliberately used as a model because it was
reminiscent of antiquity but was also intact. It was, so to
speak, a shortcut to imitating the exemplary antique.
Thereby, Günther similarly assumes that the choices of the
time were conditioned by a precise historical consciousness and an awareness of stylistic distinction.

33 Gombrich, "From the Revival of Letters" (see fn. 15): 101.

34 Ibid.: 102.

35 Ibid.: 106.

36 Burns, "Quattrocento Architecture" (see fn. 20): 276–277.

37 Onians, *Bearers of Meaning* (see fn. 20): 130–136; a recent
attempt at bridging the various explanations is offered by
Hemsoll, *Emulating Antiquity* (see fn. 21), who in his thorough analysis of Brunelleschi's architecture acknowledges
its eclectic sources, although his book remains largely
concerned with how to reconcile Brunelleschi's medieval
models with a revival of antiquity.

38 Nagel and Wood, *Anachronic Renaissance* (see fn. 11): 135.

39 Ibid.: 135–136.

40 Ibid.: 135. They argue, that Brunelleschi and Alberti were
aware that their models were post-antique, but that these
could work as a "stand in for the missing ancient models
that they really wanted"; ibid.: 142.

Ansatz eher die Projektion eines wissenschaftlichen und historisch bewussten Umgangs der Renaissance mit der Vergangenheit als eine kritische Auseinandersetzung mit dem Antikenbegriff der Renaissance. Günther legt in *Die Renaissance der Antike* nahe, dass die romanische Architektur bewusst als Vorbild herangezogen wurde, weil sie an die Antike erinnerte, aber intakt war; Günther, *Die Renaissance der Antike* (wie Anm. 24): 7. Sie ermöglichte sozusagen eine Abkürzung zur Nachahmung der vorbildhaften Antike. Damit geht auch er davon aus, dass die damaligen Entscheidungen durch ein genaues Geschichtsbewusstsein und ein Bewusstsein für stilistische Differenzierung bedingt waren.

34 Gombrich, »From the Revival of Letters« (wie Anm. 16): 101.

35 Ebd.: 102.

36 Ebd.: 106.

37 Burns, »Quattrocento Architecture« (wie Anm. 21): 276–277.

38 Onians, *Bearers of Meaning* (wie Anm. 21): 130–136 Einen rezenteren Versuch, die verschiedenen Erklärungen zu verbinden, bietet Hemsoll, *Emulating Antiquity* (wie Anm. 22). In seiner gründlichen Analyse der Architektur Brunelleschis erkennt er ihre eklektischen Quellen zwar an, das Hauptziel seines Buches besteht jedoch weiterhin darin, Brunelleschis mittelalterliche Modelle mit einer Wiederbelebung der Antike zu vereinbaren.

39 Nagel and Wood, *Anachronic Renaissance* (wie Anm. 11): 135.

40 Ebd.: 135–136.

41 Ebd.: 135. Sie argumentieren auch, dass Brunelleschi und Alberti wussten, dass ihre Modelle nachantik waren, sie jedoch davon ausgingen, dass diese als Ersatz für das fehlende antike Ideal dienen konnten: »stand in for the missing ancient models that they really wanted«; ebd.: 142.

42 *Giovanni Rucellai ed il suo Zibaldone: I, »Il Zibaldone Quaresimale«*, Alessandro Perosa et al., Hrsg. (*Studies of the Warburg Institute*, Vol. 24) (London, 1960): 61.

43 Leon Battista Alberti, *De iciarchia*, in: *Opere volgari*, C. Grayson, Hrsg., 3 Bd. (Bari 1960–1973), Bd. 2: 187; L. B.

41 *Giovanni Rucellai ed il suo Zibaldone: I, "Il Zibaldone
   Quaresimale"*, Alessandro Perosa et al., eds. (*Studies of
   the Warburg Institute,* Vol. 24) (London, 1960): 61.

42 Leon Battista Alberti, *De iciarchia*, in: *Opere volgari*,
   C. Grayson, ed., 3 vols. (Bari, 1960–1973), vol. 2: 187;
   L. B. Alberti, *Profugiorum af erumna libri*, G. Ponte, ed.,
   (Genova, 1988): 49.

43 *Sebastiano Serlio on Architecture*, books I–V of 'Tutte
   l'Opere d'architecttura et prospetiva", Vaughan Hart and
   Peter Hicks, trans. (intr. and comment.), (New Haven, CT,
   1996), book III. After the first plates with ancient Roman
   and late antique buildings, Serlio explains that, although
   initially he had presented the book as only dealing with
   antiquity, he would not refrain from adding some modern
   buildings ("cose moderne fatte a tempi nostri"), given that
   architecture had been resuscitated by Bramante to the
   level of the ancients, ibid., vol. I: 127; Francisco de Hollanda promotes the same idea, claiming that "we may also
   call [contemporary Italian painting] antique, even though
   it is done today", Francisco de Hollanda, *On Antique
   Painting*, Alice Sedgwick Wohl, trans., (University Park,
   PA, 2013): 91; Francisco de Holanda, *Da pintura antiga*,
   Angel Gonzáles Garcia (intr. and not.) (Porto, 1964): 79:
   "E o que hoje se pinta, onde se sabe pintar, que é sómente
   em Italia, podemos lhe chamar tembem antigo, sendo
   feito hoje em este dia".

44 Vasari, *Vite* (see fn. 17): 24; Manetti, *Vita* (see fn. 22): 76, on
   San Pier Scheraggio and Santi Apostoli as churches built
   by Charlemagne.

45 Vasari, *Vite* (see fn. 25): 24. In the "Life of Andrea Tafi",
   Vasari praises Santi Apostoli: "S. Apostolo di Firenze: opera
   di tanto buona maniera che tira alla vera bontà antica", *Vite*
   (see fn. 17): 74; Vasari's acknowledgement of Brunelleschi's
   medieval models is comprehensively discussed by Nagel
   and Wood, *Anachronic Renaissance* (see fn. 11): 135–146.

46 Rucellai, *Zibaldone* (see fn. 41): 68.

47 Ibid.: 74: "[...] una cappella di Sancta Chostanza, tonda, con
   colonne doppie a coppie, con begli archi, e nella volta
   bellissimi musaichi con figure piccole in perfectione et con
   fogliami et alberi et molti spiritegli che navicano in diverse

Alberti, *Profugiorum af erumna libri*, G. Ponte, Hrsg. (Genf, 1988): 49.

44 *Sebastiano Serlio on Architecture*, Books I–V of »Tutte l'Opere d'architecttura et prospetiva«, Vaughan Hart und Peter Hicks, übers. (Einleitung und Kommentar), (New Haven, CT, 1996), Buch III. Im Anschluss an die ersten Tafeln mit antik-römischen und spätantiken Bauten erklärt Serlio, dass er, entgegen seiner anfänglichen Darstellung, sich das Buch ausschließlich mit der Antike befasse und er nicht darauf verzichten könne, einige moderne Bauten (»cose moderne fatte a tempi nostri«) hinzuzufügen, da die Architektur von Bramante wieder auf das Niveau der Alten gebracht worden sei; ebd., Bd. I: 127. Francisco de Holanda verfolgt dieselbe Idee, wenn er behauptet, dass die zeitgenössische italienische Malerei auch als antik bezeichnet werden könne, obwohl sie »heute gemalt« werde: »E o que hoje se pinta, onde se sabe pintar, que é sómente em Italia, podemos lhe chamar tembem antigo, sendo feito hoje em este dia«, Francisco de Holanda, *Da pintura antiga*, Angel Gonzáles Garcia (Einleitung und Kommentar) (Porto, 1964): 79.

45 Vasari, *Vite* (wie Anm. 18): 24. Zur Attribution von San Pier Scheraggio und Santi Apostoli an Karl den Großen vgl. Manetti, *Vita* (wie Anm. 23): 76.

46 Vasari, *Vite* (wie Anm. 26): 24. In seiner Vita des Andrea Tafi lobt Vasari Santi Apostoli: »Apostolo di Firenze: opera di tanto buona maniera che tira alla vera bontà antica«, *Vite*: 74. Vasaris Anerkennung von Brunelleschis mittelalterlichen Vorbildern wird von Nagel und Wood umfassend diskutiert, *Anachronic Renaissance* (wie Anm. 11): 135–146.

47 Rucellai, *Zibaldone* (wie Anm. 42): 68.

48 Ebd.: 74: »[...] una cappella di Sancta Chostanza, tonda, con colonne doppie a coppie, con begli archi, e nella volta bellissimi musaichi con figure piccole in perfectione et con fogliami et alberi et molti spirit egli che navicano in diverse maniere, il quale è il più vacho, gratioso et gentile musaico non che di Roma, ma di tutto il mondo«.

49 Maria Fabricius Hansen, »Representing the Past: The Concept and Study of Antique Architecture in 15th-

maniere, il quale è il più vacho, gratioso et gentile musaico non che di Roma, ma di tutto il mondo".

48 Maria Fabricius Hansen, "Representing the Past: The Concept and Study of Antique Architecture in 15th-Century Italy", in: *Analecta Romana Instituti Danici* 23 (1996): 90–91.

49 Nagel and Wood, *Anachronic Renaissance* (see fn. 11): 137, list a series of examples from various Italian cities; on examples mainly from Rome, including Santo Stefano Rotondo, see Günther, *Die Renaissance der Antike* (see fn. 23): 43–45.

50 Rucellai, *Zibaldone* (see fn. 41): 69: "Item, nell'abituro dentro, uno bellissimo chiostro con colonette di marmo a coppie, con begli archi da colonna a colonna, et dal lato di fuori bellissime cornici et architravi con due fregi di fogliami et altre gentileze di musaicho, con belle tavolette et tondi di porfido, di serpentine et di granito".

51 Ibid.: 67–78. There was a readiness at the time to understand buildings in terms of corporeal metaphors, in tandem with a reluctance towards structures that were deemed too materially imposing and heavy and towards ruins that were seen as 'decaying'. Hansen, "Representing the Past" (see fn. 48): 100–104.

52 Rucellai, *Zibaldone* (see fn. 41): 100.

53 The alleged studies of Roman architecture by Brunelleschi and Donatello are described in Manetti, *Vita* (see fn. 22): 66: "[...] insieme e' levassono grossamente in disegno quasi tutti gli edifici di Roma ed in molti luoghi circustanti di fuori, colle misure delle larghezze ed altezze, secondo che potevano arbitrando, certificarsi, e longitudini ecc. E in molti luoghi facevano cavare per vedere e riscontri de' membri degli edifici e le loro qualità, s'egli erano quadri o di quanti anguli, o tondi perfetti o ovati o di che condizione [...]"; Günther, *Die Renaissance der Antike* (see fn. 23): 19, notes that hardly anything is preserved from the early studies by Brunelleschi and other artists, yet he does not question that they took place.

54 Manetti, *Vita* (see fn. 22): 63–65: "E nel guardare le scolture, come quello che aveva buono occhio ancora mentale ed aveduto in tutte le cose, vide el modo del murare degli

Century Italy«, in: *Analecta Romana Instituti Danici* 23
(1996): 90–91.

50 Für eine Liste an Beispielen aus verschiedenen italienischen Städten siehe Nagel and Wood, *Anachronic Renaissance* (wie Anm. 11): 137. Römische Beispiele inklusive
Santo Stefano Rotondo werden von Günther angeführt,
Günther, *Die Renaissance der Antike* (wie Anm. 24): 43–45.

51 Rucellai, *Zibaldone* (wie Anm. 42): 69: »Item, nell'abituro
dentro, uno bellissimo chiostro con colonette di marmo a
coppie, con begli archi da colonna a colonna, et dal lato di
fuori bellissime cornici et architravi con due fregi di fogliami et altre gentileze di musaicho, con belle tavolette et
tondi di porfido, di serpentine et di granito.«

52 Rucellai, *Zibaldone* (wie Anm. 42): 67–78. Die zeitgenössische Tendenz Gebäude anhand körperlicher Metaphern zu
verstehen, ging mit einer Abneigung gegen allzu material-
sichtige, schwere Bauten und Ruinen einher, deren Verfall
negativ konnotiert war. Hansen, »Representing the Past«
(wie Anm. 49): 100–104.

53 Rucellai, *Zibaldone* (wie Anm. 42): 100.

54 Brunelleschis und Donatellos angebliche Studien antik-
römischer Architektur werden von Manetti beschrieben:
»[...]insieme e' levassono grossamente in disegno quasi tutti
gli edifici di Roma ed in molti luoghi circustanti di fuori,
colle misure delle larghezze ed altezze, secondo che potevano arbitrando, certificarsi, e longitudini ecc. E in molti
luoghi facevano cavare per vedere e riscontri de' membri
degli edifici e le loro qualità, s'egli erano quadri o di quanti
anguli, o tondi perfetti o ovati o di che condizione [...]«,
Manetti, *Vita* (wie Anm. 23): 66. Günther merkt dazu an,
dass »kaum« etwas von den frühen Studien Brunelleschis
und anderer erhalten sei, stellt diese jedoch nicht in Frage.
Günther, *Die Renaissance der Antike* (wie Anm. 24): 19.

55 Manetti, *Vita* (wie Anm. 23): 63–65: »E nel guardare le
scolture, come quello che aveva buono occhio ancora
mentale ed aveduto in tutte le cose, vide el modo del murare degli antichi e le loro simetrie, e parvegli conoscere un
certo ordine di membri e d'ossa«.

56 Ebd.: 66: »[...] e Donatello sanza mai aprire gli occhi alla
architettura, e Filippo non gli comunicò mai tale pensiero,

antichi e le loro simetrie, e parvegli conoscere un certo
ordine di membri e d'ossa [...]".

55 Ibid.: 66: "[...] e Donatello sanza mai aprire gli occhi alla
architettura, e Filippo non gli comunicò mai tale pensiero,
o perché e' non vi vedesse atto Donato, o forse si difidava
di non giugnere tali cose, veggendo a ogni ora più le sue
dificultà [...]"; Manetti's description of their architectural
investigations and excavations is quoted above, see fn. 54.

56 Francesco di Giorgio Martini, *Trattati di architettura,
ingegneria e arte militare*, Corrado Maltese, ed., 2 vols.
(Milan, 1967); *Il libro di Giuliano da Sangallo: Codice
Vaticano Barberiniano Latino 4424*, Cristiano Huelsen, ed.,
2 vols. (Leipzig, 1910).

57 Tilman Buddensieg, "Criticism and Praise of the Pantheon
in the Middle Ages and the Renaissance", in: R. R. Bolgar.,
ed., *Classical Influences on European Culture A.D. 500–1500*,
(Cambridge, 1976): 263–265.

58 Ibid.: 259–267.

59 "Criticism of Ancient Architecture in the Sixteenth and
Seventeenth Centuries", in: R. R. Bolgar, ed., *Classical Influences on European Culture A.D. 1500–1700* (Cambridge,
1976): 335–348; Günther, *Das Studium* (see fn. 23): 300.
Similarly observes that Serlio orders the architectural
material to a degree unknown to Vitruvius: „Dies System
entlehnt seine einzelnen Elemente zumeist Vitruv, aber die
formale Geschlossenheit und logische Konsequenz, die es
anstrebt, kennt Vitruv so nicht. Sie entsprechen überhaupt
mehr dem Geist der Renaissance als der Antike"; cf. the
observations, in: Onians, *Bearers of Meaning* (see fn. 20):
148–149, concerning Alberti's medieval sources and – parallel to this – his rejections of Vitruvius.

60 Günther, *Das Studium* (see fn. 23): 319.

61 Raphael's letter is quoted from "Appendix I: Letter from
Raphael to Pope Leo X, drafted by Angelo Colocci, with
Annotation by Raphael. Munich, Bayerische Staatsbibliothek, Cod. It. 37b", in: Ingrid D. Rowland, "Raphael, Angelo Colocci, and the Genesis of the Architectural Orders",
in: *Art Bulletin* 76 (1994): 100; "[...] havendomi Vostra Santità comandato che io ponessi in designo Roma anticha,
quanto cognoscier si può per quello che oggidì si vede [...]".

o perché e' non vi vedesse atto Donato, o forse si difidava di non giugnere tali cose, veggendo a ogni ora più le sue dificultà.« Für Manettis Beschreibung der Architektur-studien und Ausgrabungen vgl. Anm. 55.

57 Francesco di Giorgio Martini, *Trattati di architettura, ingegneria e arte militare*, Corrado Maltese, Hrsg., 2 Bd. (Mailand, 1967) und *Il libro di Giuliano da Sangallo: Codice Vaticano Barberiniano Latino 4424*, Cristiano Huelsen, Hrsg., 2 Bd. (Leipzig, 1910).

58 Tilman Buddensieg, »Criticism and Praise of the Pantheon in the Middle Ages and the Renaissance«, in: R. R. Bolgar, Hrsg., *Classical Influences on European Culture A. D. 500–1500* (Cambridge, 1976): 263–265.

59 Ebd.: 259–267.

60 Ebd.: 335–348. Günther stellt fest, dass Serlio die Elemente der römischen Architektur in einem Ausmaß systemati-sierte, das Vitruv völlig unbekannt war: »Dies System entlehnt seine einzelnen Elemente zumeist Vitruv, aber die formale Geschlossenheit und logische Konsequenz, die es anstrebt, kennt Vitruv so nicht. Sie entsprechen überhaupt mehr dem Geist der Renaissance als der Antike«, Günther, *Das Studium* (wie Anm. 24): 300. Onians Beobachtungen zu Albertis mittelalterlichen Quellen und seiner Ablehnung Vitruvs sind in diesem Zusammenhang erwähnenswert: Onians, *Bearers of Meaning* (wie Anm. 21): 148–149.

61 Günther, *Das Studium* (wie Anm. 24): 319.

62 »[...] havendomi Vostra Santità comandato che io ponessi in designo Roma anticha, quanto cognoscier si può per quello che oggidì si vede [...]«; Originalzitate des Briefes nach: »Appendix I: Letter from Raphael to Pope Leo X, drafted by Angelo Colocci, with Annotations by Raphael. Munich, Bayerische Staatsbibliothek, Cod. It. 37b«, in: Ingrid D. Rowland, »Raphael, Angelo Colocci, and the Genesis of the Architectural Orders«, in: *Art Bulletin* 76 (1994): 81–104, hier 100.

63 »Brief an Papst Leo X. betreffend die Bewahrung, Vermes-sung und zeichnerische Aufnahme der antiken Baudenk-maler Roms [um 1518]«, Peter Heinrich Jahn und Michael Cuntz, Übers., in: *Zeitschrift für Medien- und Kulturfor-schung (Schwerpunkt Entwerfen)*, Heft I, 2012: 76.

62 The English translation is in "Appendix: The Letter to
    Leo X by Raphael and Baldassare Castiglione (*c.* 1519)", in:
    Vaughan Hart & Peter Hicks, *Palladio's Rome: A Translation
    of Andrea Palladio's Two Guidebooks to Rome* (New Haven,
    CT, 2006): 182.

63 Rowland, "Raphael" (see fn. 61): 101.

64 Ibid.; English translation in "The Letter to Leo X" (see
    fn. 62): 185: "Nor is there any difficulty in telling our mod-
    ern buildings apart from Gothic ones, If for no other reason
    than their newness, by which they are very recognizable".

65 Rowland, "Raphael" (see fn. 61): 101: "Perche di tre maniere
    di edifici solamente si ritrovano in Roma, delle quali la una
    e di quelli buoni antichi, che durorno dalli primi Impera-
    tori sino al tempo che Roma fu ruinata e guasta dalli gotti
    e da altri Barbari".

66 Ibid.: "L'altra Durò tanto che roma fu dominata da' Gotti e
    anchora Cento anni di poi".

67 Ibid.: "L'altra, da quel tempo sino alli tempi nostri".

68 Panofsky, *Renaissance and Renascences* (see fn. 4): 24, n. 1.

69 Rowland, "Raphael" (see fn. 61): 101–102.

70 Ibid.: 102: "parete di fuora" and "parete di dentro". He also
    defines the section: "It shows the inside of the building –
    half, that is, as if cut down the middle". English translation
    in: "The Letter to Leo X" (see fn. 62): 189.

71 Ibid.: 190–191.Raphael noted here, that this was a manner
    of drawing used by painters but useful to architects, as well.

72 Ibid.: 188: "The plan is what compartitions the whole of
    the 'flat' area of the place where one is to build – what they
    mean is the drawing of the base of the whole building
    when it is still close to the level of the ground. This area,
    even if it were sloping, would be rendered flat, and you
    should make sure that the horizontal line at the base of the
    slope and the area that was rendered level are parallel with
    all the other levels of the building. […] this plan encom-
    passes the base area of the entire building, just as the sole
    of the foot encompasses the space that is the foundation of
    the whole body".

73 See, for instance: Antonio Averlino detto il Filarete,
    Trattato di architettura, Anna Maria Finoli e Liliana Grassi,
    eds., 2 vols., (Milan, 1972), vol. 2, Tav. 55 (fol. 78 v).

64 Rowland, »Raphael« (wie Anm. 62): 101.

65 Ebd. und »Brief an Papst Leo X« (wie Anm. 63): 76: »Die demnach modernen und aus unserer Epoche stammenden Gebäude sind allseits bekannt, indem sie neu sind [...].«

66 »Perche di tre maniere di edifici solamente si ritrovano in Roma, delle quali la una e di quelli buoni antichi, che durorno dalli primi Imperatori sino al tempo che Roma fu ruinata e guasta dalli gotti e da altri Barbari...«, Rowland, »Raphael« (wie Anm. 62): 101.

67 Ebd.: »L'altra Durò tanto che roma fu dominata da' Gotti e anchora Cento anni di poi«.

68 Ebd.: »L'altra, da quel tempo sino alli tempi nostri«.

69 Panofsky, *Renaissance and Renascences* (wie Anm. 4): 24, Anm. 1.

70 Rowland, »Raphael« (wie Anm. 62): 101–102.

71 Ebd.: 102: »Parete di fuora« und »parete di dentro«. Raffael definiert auch den Schnitt: »Und dieser [...] zeigt die innere Hälfte des Gebäudes, als ob es in der Mitte geteilt wäre.«; »Brief an Papst Leo X« (wie Anm. 63): 84.

72 Ebd.: 82. Zu den Perspektivzeichnungen merkt Raffael an, dass diese der Praxis der Malerei entstammen, jedoch auch für Architekten nützlich seien.

73 Ebd.: »Der Grundriss ist jener, welcher das ganze ebene Areal des Bauplatzes einteilt, oder, anders gesagt, die Zeichnung des gesamten Gebäudefundamentes, wenn es bereits das Oberflächenniveau des Erdbodens erreicht hat. Selbst wenn das entsprechende Areal auf einem Berg liegt, muss es auf eine ebene Fläche übertragen werden, und es muss bewerkstelligt werden, dass die Grundlinie des Berges zur jeweiligen Grundlinie der Gebäudeniveaus parallel ist. Und um dies zu erreichen, muss man die eben verlaufende Linie am Fuß des Berges erfassen und nicht die Umrisslinie in der Höhe, so dass über ersterer alle Mauern ins Lot fallen und senkrecht stehen. Und man nennt diese Zeichnung Grundriss, weil, vergleichbar der Fläche, welche die Fußsohle als Fundament des menschlichen Körpers einnimmt, so dieser Grundriss das Fundament des gesamten Gebäudes ist«.

74 Antonio Averlino detto il Filarete, *Trattato di architettura*, Anna Maria Finoli e Liliana Grassi, Hg., 2 Bd., (Mailand, 1972), 2. Bd., Tav. 55 (Fol. 78 v).

74 English translation in "The Letter to Leo X" (see fn. 62): 189. Italian in Rowland, "Raphael" (see fn. 61): 102: "El che è necessario a tal artificio, che rircerca tutte le misure perfette in facto, et tirate con linee paralelle, non con quelle che paiono, e non sono [...]".

75 English translation in "The Letter to Leo X" (see fn. 62): 181. Italian in Rowland, "Raphael" (see fn. 61): 100: "[...] che per vero argumento si possono infallibilmente ridurre nel termine proprio come stavano [...]".

76 Richard Krautheimer, "Introduction to an 'Iconography of Mediaeval Architecture'", in: *Journal of the Warburg and Courtauld Institutes* 5 (1942): 1–33.

77 Pliny, *Natural History*, D. E. Eichholz, trans., (Loeb Classical Library), vol. X (Cambridge, MA, 1962). XXXVI.xvii.80. Pliny continued this presentation with the measurements of the second and third largest pyramids, and only after relaying this information about the measurements of the third pyramid did he find it relevant to add, that it had "sloping sides between the corners".

78 I am grateful to Professor Emeritus, Jesper Lützen, University of Copenhagen, for information on the history of mathematics; the inexistent idea of accuracy is succinctly described in Alexandre Koyré, "Du monde de l'à-peu-près' à l'univers de la précision" (1948), in: Études d'histoire de la pensée philosophique (*Cahiers des Annales*, 19) (Paris, 1961): 311–329. Who argues, however, that notions of accuracy began to advance in the second half of the sixteenth century, going hand in hand with technological innovations, and that modern notions of accuracy finally became manifest in the eighteenth century; Günther, *Das Studium*: 62 (see fn. 23), observes that around 1500 there existed no standardization of measuring units, and even Peruzzi, Antonio da Sangallo, and others involved in Raphael's project of reconstructing Rome (c. 1518–1520) produced drawings with different units of measurement.

79 Leon Battista Alberti, *On the Art of Building in Ten Books*, J. Rykwert, N. Leach & R. Tavernor, trans., (Cambridge, MA, 1988), VII: 4: 196.

80 Hubertus Günther, „Das Buch über die Säulenordnungen", in: Dietrich Erben, ed., *Das Buch als Entwurf: Textgattungen*

75 »Brief an Papst Leo X« (wie Anm. 63): 83. Im Original: »El che è necessario a tal artificio, che rircerca tutte le misure perfette in facto, et tirate con linee paralelle, non con quelle che paiono, e non sono [...].« Rowland, »Raphael« (wie Anm. 62): 102.

76 »Brief an Papst Leo X« (wie Anm. 63): 76. Im Original: »[...] che per vero argumento si possono infallibilmente ridurre nel termine proprio come stavano [...].« Rowland, »Raphael« (wie Anm. 62): 100.

77 Richard Krautheimer, »Introduction to an ›Iconography of Mediaeval Architecture‹«, in: *Journal of the Warburg and Courtauld Institutes* 5 (1942): 1–33.

78 Pliny, *Natural History*, D. E. Eichholz, Übers., (Loeb Classical Library), Vol. X (Cambridge, MA, 1962) XXXVI.xvii.80. Plinius setzte diese Darstellung mit den Maßen der zweit- und drittgrößten Pyramide fort, und erst nach seinen Angaben zu den Maßen der dritten Pyramide merkt er an, dass diese »schräge Seiten zwischen den Ecken« hatte.

79 Ich danke Prof. Emeritus Jesper Lützen von der Universität Kopenhagen für Informationen zur Geschichte der Mathematik; die inexistente Idee der Genauigkeit ist kurz und bündig beschrieben in Alexandre Koyré, »Du monde de l'à-peu-près' à l'univers de la précision« [1948], in: *Études d'histoire de la pensée philosophique* (*Cahiers des Annales*, 19) (Paris, 1961): 311–329. Koyré argumentiert jedoch, dass sich die Vorstellungen von Genauigkeit in der zweiten Hälfte des 16. Jahrhunderts parallel zu den technischen Neuerungen zu entwickeln begannen und dass sich der moderne Genauigkeitsbegriff schließlich im 18. Jahrhundert durchgesetzt habe. Hubertus Günther stellt dagegen fest, dass es um 1500 keine Standardisierung der Maßeinheiten gab und selbst Peruzzi, Antonio da Sangallo und andere, die an Raffaels Projekt der Rekonstruktion Roms um 1518–1520 beteiligt waren, Zeichnungen mit unterschiedlichen Maßeinheiten schufen. Günther, *Das Studium* (wie Anm. 24): 62.

80 Leon Battista Alberti, *Zehn Bücher über die Baukunst*, Max Theuer, Übers. und Hrsg. (Wien, 1912) VII: 4: 353.

81 Hubertus Günther, »Das Buch über die Säulenordnungen«, in: Dietrich Erben, Hrsg., *Das Buch als Entwurf: Textgattun-*

in der Geschichte der Architekturtheorie. Ein Handbuch (Paderborn, 2019): 94–128.

81 Rowland, "Raphael" (see fn. 61): 103. On the novelty of the term 'orders', see Rowland, "Raphael" (see fn. 61): 81–104 and Onians, *Bearers of Meaning* (see fn. 20): 247–248.

82 An obsession with the orders took hold around 1500 and was not shared by architects of the early fifteenth century; see Burns, "Quattrocento Architecture" (see fn. 20): 276, 286–287.

83 See fn. 24.

84 Saalman, "Capital Studies" (see fn. 24).

85 Filarete, *Trattato* (see fn. 73); Francesco di Giorgio Martini, *Trattati* (see fn. 56); the foundational work on the uses and meanings of columns and capitals from antiquity until the sixteenth century remains Onians, *Bearers of Meaning* (see fn. 20).

86 Burns, "Quattrocento Architecture" (see fn. 20): 276; in addition to the illustrations in Filarete's and Francesco di Giorgio's manuscripts, Giuliano da Sangallo's great *Codex Barberini*, compiled in the early sixteenth century, is a major source concerning this interest in capitals (see fn. 56).

87 Ingrid D. Rowland, "Translator's Preface", in: Vitruvius: *Ten Books on Architecture*, I.D. Rowland, trans., Thomas Noble Howe (comment. and ill.), I.D. Rowland & Michael J. Dewar (additional comment.), (Cambridge, 1999): xiii–xiv.

88 Alberti, *On the Art of Building*, VI: 1 (see fn. 79): 154–155.

89 *Sebastiano Serlio on Architecture*, book IV, fol. 127 (see fn. 43): 255.

90 Rowland, "Raphael" (see fn. 61): 103.

91 Vasari, *Vite* (see fn. 17): 3–32.

92 Ibid.: 3–4.

93 Willibald Sauerländer, "From Stilus to Style. Reflections on the Fate of a Notion", in: *Art History* 6 (1983): 259–261 and Reinhart Koselleck, *Vergangene Zukunft: Zur Semantik geschichtlicher Zeiten* (Frankfurt am Main, 1979) [1984]: 17–37.

94 Sauerländer, "From Stilus to Style" (see fn. 93): 257; John Shearman, *Mannerism* (Harmondsworth, 1967): 15–48.

gen in der Geschichte der Architekturtheorie. Ein Handbuch (Paderborn, 2019): 94–128.

82 Rowland, »Raphael« (wie Anm. 62): 103. Zur Konzeptualisierung der Säulenordnungen auch Rowland, »Raphael«: 81–104 und Onians, *Bearers of Meaning* (wie Anm. 21): 247–248.

83 Die für die Zeit um 1500 typische Obsession mit den Säulenordnungen wurde von den Architekten des frühen 15. Jahrhunderts nicht geteilt; vgl. Burns, »Quattrocento Architecture« (wie Anm. 21): 276, 286–287.

84 Vgl. Anm. 25.

85 Saalman, »Capital Studies« (wie Anm. 25).

86 Vgl. Filarete, *Trattato* (wie Anm. 74) und Francesco di Giorgio Martini, *Trattati* (wie Anm. 57). Die grundlegende Studie zum Bedeutungswandel von Säulen und Kapitellen von der Antike ins 16. Jahrhundert ist Onians, *Bearers of Meaning* (wie Anm. 21).

87 Burns, »Quattrocento Architecture« (wie Anm. 21): 276. Neben den illustrierten Manuskripten Filaretes und Francesco di Giorgios kann Giuliano da Sangallos monumentaler *Codex Barberini*, der im frühen 16. Jahrhundert kompiliert wurde, als bedeutende Quelle für das neue Interesse an Kapitellen genannt werden (wie Anm. 57).

88 Ingrid D. Rowland, »Translator's Preface«, in: Vitruvius: *Ten Books on Architecture*, I. D. Rowland, Übers., Thomas Noble Howe (Kommentar und Ill.), I. D. Rowland und Michael J. Dewar (Zusatzkommentar), (Cambridge, 1999): xiii–xiv.

89 Alberti, *On the Art of Building*, VI: 1 (wie Anm. 80): 154–155.

90 *Sebastiano Serlio on Architecture*, book IV, fol. 127 (wie Anm. 44): 255.

91 Rowland, »Raphael« (wie Anm. 62): 103.

92 Vasari, *Vite* (wie Anm. 18): 3–32.

93 Ebd.: 3–4.

94 Willibald Sauerländer, »From Stilus to Style. Reflections on the Fate of a Notion«, in: *Art History* 6 (1983), 259–261 und Reinhart Koselleck, *Vergangene Zukunft: Zur Semantik geschichtlicher Zeiten* (Frankfurt am Main, 1979) [1984]: 17–37.

95 On the concept of style in the sixteenth century as independent of national and geographic categories, which only become manifest in the modern art-historical discipline, see Stephen J. Campbell, *The Endless Periphery: Toward a Geopolitics of Art in Lorenzo Lotto's Italy* (Chicago, IL, 2019): 44–47. On early approaches to stylistic-chronological comparisons in studies of ancient coins by contemporaries of Vasari, see Ulrich Pfisterer, *Lysippus und seine Freunde: Liebesgaben und Gedächtnis im Rom der Renaissance oder: Das erste Jahrhundert der Medaille* (Berlin, 2008): 165–168.

96 Rowland, "Raphael" (see fn. 61): 101: "schiochissime, senza arte o disegno alcuno [...]"; Sauerländer, "From Stilus to Style" (see fn. 93); for a concise survey of the precursors to the modern practice of associating a given period with a given style, see Ulrich Pfisterer, „Epochenstil", in: *Donatello* (see fn. 12): 79–91.

97 Wölfflin, *Principles of Art History* (see fn. 3): 93.

95 Sauerländer, »From Stilus to Style« (wie Anm. 94): 257;
John Shearman, *Mannerism* (Harmondsworth, 1967): 15–48.

96 Zur Konzeptualisierung von Stil im 16. Jahrhundert, die
noch unabhängig von jenen nationalen und geografischen
Kategorien war, die erst in der modernen kunsthistori-
schen Disziplin relevant werden sollten, Stephen J. Camp-
bell, *The Endless Periphery: Toward a Geopolitics of Art in
Lorenzo Lotto's Italy* (Chicago, 2019): 44–47. Zu frühen
Versuchen stilistischer und chronologischer Vergleiche in
Studien antiker Münzen zur Zeit Vasaris siehe Ulrich
Pfisterer, *Lysippus und seine Freunde: Liebesgaben und
Gedächtnis im Rom der Renaissance, oder Das erste Jahrhun-
dert der Medaille* (Berlin, 2008): 165–168.

97 Rowland, »Raphael« (wie Anm. 62): 101: »[...] schiochissime,
senza arte o disegno alcuno [...]«. Einen kurzen Überblick
zu Vorläufern des modernen Konzepts der Verknüpfung
von Epochen und Stilen gibt Ulrich Pfisterer, »Epochenstil«, in *Donatello* (wie Anm. 13): 79–91.

98 Wölfflin, *Kunstgeschichtliche Grundbegriffe* (wie Anm. 3): 12.

Abbildungsnachweis Illustrations:

Abb. 1, 15: Wikimedia Commons / Abb. 2: CC BY-SA 4.0 Wikimedia Commons, photo: FrDr / Abb. 3: Unsplash, photo: Gabriella Clare Marino / Abb. 4: Wikimedia Commons / Abb. 5: Scan aus: Serlio, Sebastiano: *Il terzo libro di Sebastiano Serlio Bolognese, nel qual si figurano. E descrivono le antiquita di Roma & le altre chesono in Italia, e fuori d'Italia*, Venetia 1540, S. 9 / Abb. 6: Nationalmuseum in Krakau / Abb. 7: CC BY-SA 3.0 Wikimedia Commons, photo: Warburg / Abb. 8: CC BY 3.0 Wikimedia Commons, photo: Alexandru Cosereanu / Abb. 9: CC BY-SA 4.0 Wikimedia Commons, photo: Benjamín Núñez González (Ausschnitt/zugeschnitten) / Abb. 10: CC BY-SA 3.0 Wikimedia Commons, photo: Lucarelli / Abb. 11: CC BY-SA 3.0 Wikimedia Commons, photo: Gryffindor / Abb. 12: Wikimedia Commons / Abb. 13, 14: © Museo del Duomo di Opera Firenze / Abb. 16: Scan aus: Francesco di Giorgio Martini, *Trattati*, Vol. 1, Tav. 163 / Turin Biblioteca Nationale / Abb. 17: Wikimedia Commons / Abb. 18: Museum Boijmans Van Beuningen / Abb. 19: Emiliani, Andrea (Hrsg.): *Amico Aspertini 1474–1552. Artista bizzarro nell'età di Dürer e Raffaello*, Mailand 2008, S. 296 und Schweikhart, Gunther: *Der Codex Wolfegg. Zeichnungen nach der Antike von Amico Aspertini*, London 1986, TAF. XV, Abb. 25 / Abb. 20: Scan aus: Francesco di Giorgio Martini, *Trattati*, Vol. 1, Tav. 147 / Abb. 21: Internet Archive/Getty Research Institute / Abb. 22: Filarete (Antonio di Piero Averlino) /John R. Spencer: *Filarete's Treatise on Architecture*, Vol. 2: The Facsimile, New Haven 1965, book XI, fol. 78v / Abb. 23, 24: Scan aus: *Il libro di Giuliano da Sangallo: Codice Vaticano Barberiniano Latino 4424*, Cristiano Huelsen, 2 vols., Leipzig 1910 / Abb. 25: Scan aus: Serlio, Sebastiano: *Regole Generali Di Architetvra Sopra Le Cinqve Maniere De Gli Edifici, Cioè, Thoscano, Dorico, Ionico, Corinthio, Et Composito, Con Gli Essempi Dell'Antiqvita, Che, Per La Magior Parte Concordano Con La Dottrina Di Vitrvvio*, Venedig 1537, S. VI

Abb. Seite 12/13: Ausschnitt aus Abb. 14, Seite 52

Umschlagabbildung Cover illustration:
  Jaana Frangini

Herausgeber Editor:
  Ulrich Pfisterer
Lektorat deutsch Copyeditor of the German texts:
  Lavinia Hunder, Leon Krause
Lektorat englisch Copyeditor of the English texts:
  Julia Oswald
Übersetzung englisch–deutsch Translation English – German:
  Konrad Krčal
Übersetzung deutsch–englisch (Vorwort) Translation German–English
(Preface):
  Julia Oswald
Gestaltung, Satz und Layout Design, type setting, and layout:
  Edgar Endl, booklab GmbH, München
Druck und Bindung Printing and binding:
  Beltz Grafische Betriebe GmbH, Bad Langensalza

Bibliografische Information der Deutschen Nationalbibliothek:
Die Deutsche Nationalbibliothek verzeichnet diese Publikation in der
Deutschen Nationalbibliografie; detaillierte bibliografische Daten
sind im Internet über http://dnb.dnb.de abrufbar.
Bibliographic information published by the Deutsche Nationalbibliothek:
The Deutsche Nationalbibliothek lists this publication in the Deutsche
Nationalbibliografie; detailed bibliographic data are available on the
Internet at http://dnb.dnb.de.

ISBN 978-3-422-80252-0
e-ISBN (PDF) 978-3-422-80268-1

Library of Congress Control Number: 2024941825